Micro Mindfulness

Mindful Practices Workbook

Easy Everyday Mindfulness

Mindful Practices

Workbook

SHIRLEY BLANCH

ISBN: 978-1-7396110-1-9

Edited and produced by: Deborah Taylor, Book-Launch Your Business
https://www.booklaunchyourbusiness.com/

Page design and layout by: Catherine Williams
https://www.chapter-one-book-production.co.uk

Cover design: Andy Prior
http://andypriordesign.co.uk/

FREE RESOURCES
Get the free mindfulness hack reminders and make mindfulness part of your everyday life.
www.getmindful.co.uk

Disclaimer
The information given in this book should not be treated as a substitute for counselling; therapy; medical; legal; psychological or any kind of professional advice. Always consult a medical practitioner. Any use of information in this book is at the reader's discretion and risk. The author cannot be held responsible for any loss, claim or damage arising out of the use, or misuse of the suggestions made, the failure to take medical advice or for any material on third party websites.

INTRODUCTION TO THE MICRO MINDFULNESS SERIES

Micro Mindfulness: Mini Mindful Hacks

This book provides a comprehensive introduction to mindfulness. It also includes micro-practices you can use throughout your day, helping you reduce stress and take back control of your life. As well as an introduction to what mindfulness is and how it can help you, the book gives you exercises you can do in the morning, at midday and in the evening – and all without any need for meditation!

Micro Mindfulness: Mindful Practices Workbook

This workbook has been designed to extend the micro mindful techniques in the main book *Micro Mindfulness: Mini Mindful Hacks*. The aim is to help you integrate the techniques into your day, so you can make mindfulness a habit that you can practise automatically.

Micro Mindfulness: Intention Setting Journal

The journal aims to help develop a daily journalling practice to help reduce stress and improve wellbeing. It can be used for intention setting practice, which can be done in the morning and as part of reflective evening practice. The *Micro-Mindfulness: Intention Setting Journal* can be used as a standalone journal or alongside the other books in this series.

CONTENTS

INTRODUCTION

Welcome to the *Micro-Mindfulness: Mindful Practices Workbook*, which has been designed to accompany the book, *Micro Mindfulness: Mini Mindful Hacks* and provides practical exercises to help you learn and put in place new, more supportive and more mindful habits.

WHY USE THIS WORKBOOK?

In my experience, combining different types of written practice is the most effective way to develop a mindful routine, which is what this workbook is designed to do. It offers the perfect opportunity to learn and practise the micro mindful techniques included in the *Micro Mindfulness: Mini Mindful Hacks* guide. I'm also a big fan of journalling, which is why it's covered here as well as in the accompanying *Micro Mindfulness: Intention Setting Journal*. The aim with the journalling pages in the workbook is to help you develop a regular daily journalling practice.

HOW THESE EXERCISES AID MINDFULNESS

The exercises in this workbook help deepen everyday mindful living by bringing awareness to the triggers and blocks you deal with daily without noticing them or realising how they affect your life. They encourage you to become the observer of your experiences, helping you to understand what causes you stress and what brings you joy so you can get a better understanding of who you are. Developing a greater understanding of your triggers and blocks allows you to develop strategies to overcome them – and that's truly transformational.

Some of the exercises are best done in the morning when you're planning your day and others work best in the evening when you're processing your day before going to sleep. This is why the exercises have been divided into Motivated Mornings and Reflective Evenings. In the final section of the workbook, they're collated into the journalling section called Bringing It All Together. You can turn this into an ongoing practice by using the *Micro Mindfulness: Intention Setting Journal.*

HOW THE EXERCISES WORK TOGETHER

In order to develop a good personal wellbeing practice, you need to know which tools to use and when, which is why these exercises have been divided into three sections:

- Foundation Exercises
- Habit-forming exercises
- Ongoing practices

Foundation exercises

All great habits need a solid foundation and these exercises provide that for your personal wellbeing practice. They help you identify personal triggers and motivators while also offering helpful 'go-to' tools you can use over and over again.

Habit-forming exercises

Habit-forming exercises have to be practised regularly over a number of days or weeks until you've learned the new behaviours and integrated them into your daily routine. You won't need to do the exercises long term because once they've become established, they'll be habits you do without thinking.

Ongoing practices

Ongoing practices such as intention setting and reflective journalling are great tools for helping you to create the life you want, so you may want to adopt these as part of your long-term mindfulness practice as they'll help you live more intentionally and process your daily experiences more mindfully.

IS PREVIOUS MINDFULNESS EXPERIENCE NECESSARY?

No, it isn't. The exercises in this workbook have been designed to encourage you to develop greater mindful awareness as part of your life and help you understand how powerful mindfulness practice can be, but there is no requirement for you to understand or practice mindfulness before you go through this workbook. If you do want to deepen your understanding of mindfulness, this is covered in more depth in the book, *Micro Mindfulness: Mini Mindful Hacks*.

IT'S ALL ABOUT YOU!

It's important to remember with any self-development work that it's about you. If a practice doesn't sit right with you for some reason, just adapt it. If you feel more comfortable using different words then use them. This is about using the tools to kick off a new more mindful way of living; one that works for YOU! If a particular practice makes you feel stressed, skip it or come back to it when you're ready.

No matter where you're starting and where you hope to get to, I wish you all the best on this journey towards a more mindful life and I hope this book takes you wherever you wish to go.

Please remember...

The mindful practices outlined in this workbook are just tools you can use to live a more mindful life. They are not intended as a replacement for counselling or therapy and the advice given here does not constitute any kind of medical, psychological, legal or professional advice.

PART ONE

MOTIVATED MORNINGS

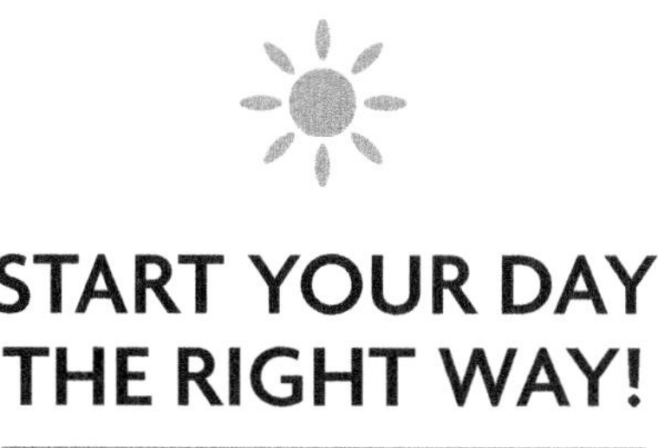

START YOUR DAY THE RIGHT WAY!

EXERCISE CHECKLIST

These exercises have been designed to help you set positive intentions so you can stay motivated and on track during your day.

Foundation Exercises

1. Emotional Scale
2. Values
3. Affirmations
4. Stress Diary

Habit-forming exercises

5. Morning Reflection
6. Mindful Awareness Planning
7. Positive Focus Tracker

Ongoing practices

8. Intention Setting Journal
9. 21 Days of Gratitude (Evening Reflection)
10. Reflective Journal (Evening Reflection)

FOUNDATION EXERCISES

These exercises form the basis of your micro mindful practice. They include Emotional Scaling, Values and Affirmations. The Stress Diary is for occasional use.

1. Emotional Scale Charts

Emotional Scale Charts are visual tools that allow you to get a clearer picture of your emotional state. The scale helps you acknowledge your feelings by writing them out on a scale that ranges from high to low. When you're in a higher emotional state, such as peace or joy, you have more energy and feel motivated. By contrast, when you're in a lower emotional state such as grief or despair, you may find you have less energy and feel drained.

It's important to remember that there are no good or bad emotions; each is appropriate depending on what's happening in your life. However, sometimes you can get stuck in a low-energy state. This is when an Emotional Scale Chart can help you see how you're feeling so you can take steps to change it. Mindfulness encourages you to notice your emotional responses to events and situations and observe them without judgement so you can release lower energy emotions rather than suppressing them.

How does an Emotional Scale Chart help?

An emotional scale encourages us to look at our emotions in terms of high or low energy, accept where we are and set a goal of where we'd like to get to. Sometimes it's hard to put a name to an emotion, especially if we weren't encouraged to talk about our feelings when we were young, so seeing emotions written down on a chart helps us to recognise which ones we are experiencing and why we might find ourselves lacking in energy.

How to use an Emotional Scale Chart

It's easy to incorporate using an emotional scale on a daily basis by simply looking at it first thing in the morning, recognising where you are and then setting yourself a goal of where you want to get to. Then you can check in with it at different times of the day to keep reminding yourself to stay on track. Words actually change our brains, so even just by mindfully focusing on the words relating to the emotions we can often notice that we feel more in alignment with that emotion.

TIP: Depending on the words you focus on, your emotional response to events in your day can feel either positive or negative, so be mindful of where you put your attention.

How to complete the Emotional Scale Chart

1. Label the arrows
   Begin by labelling the arrows to reflect different energy levels.
   - Label the arrow pointing up **HIGH ENERGY**, as in the example on page 10. Alternatively, you can use a different high energy word if you prefer, e.g. **motivated**, **creative**, **empowered**, etc.
   - Label the arrow pointing down **LOW ENERGY** as in the example on page 10. As before, you can use another low energy word if you prefer, e.g. **demotivated**, **powerless**, **stuck** etc.

Why this works

Dividing emotions into high vs low stops us labelling them as good or bad which can lead us into judgement/suppression of emotions. This encourages us to take a more mindful approach, understanding that we can notice our emotional experiences and allow them to come and go without judgement.

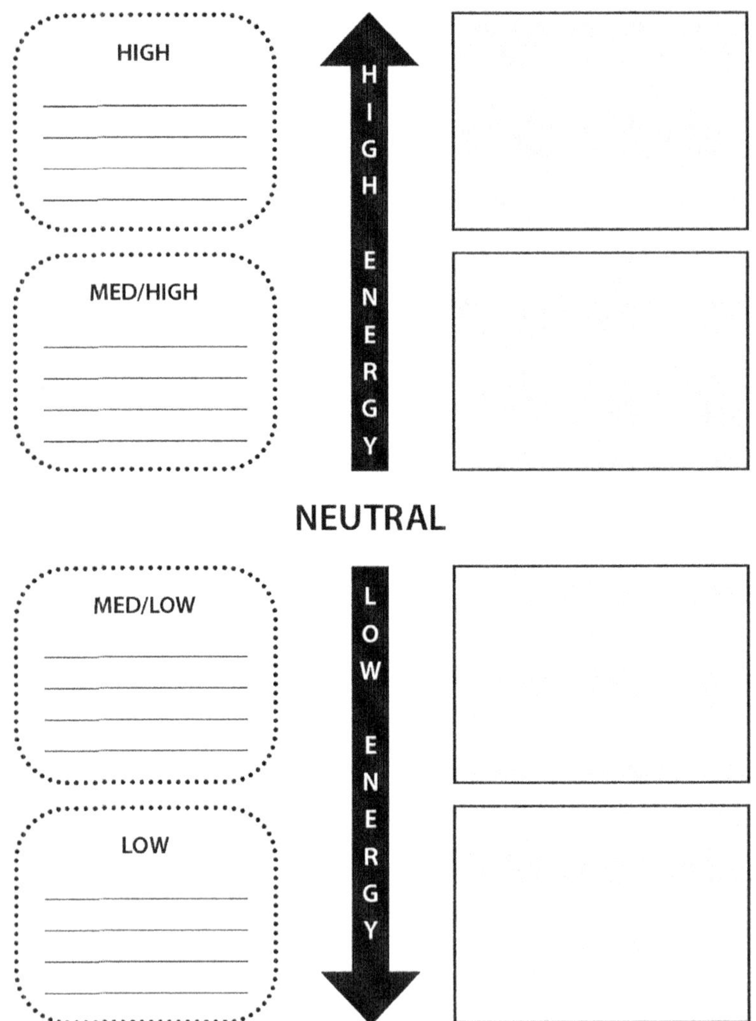

2. Describe your emotions
   On the lines to the left of the arrows, add 16 words (four in each section) to describe how you feel. Use the higher and lower energy emotion word lists as a guide (see pages 12-13). Start from the top, dividing your words into four emotional levels:

   HIGH; MEDIUM/HIGH; MEDIUM/LOW; LOW

   Use words that resonate and feel right to you.

- The higher energy emotions are those you experience on days when you can't wait to jump out of bed and start your day.
- The lower energy emotions will be those you feel when you're at your lowest point, such as when you're struggling to drag yourself out of bed in the morning.

Why this works

Creating an emotional scale encourages us to bring a new level of awareness to what we are feeling and to the language we use to describe our emotions. When we do this, it expands our vocabulary around our feelings, which helps us express ourselves better and leads to improved communication with others.

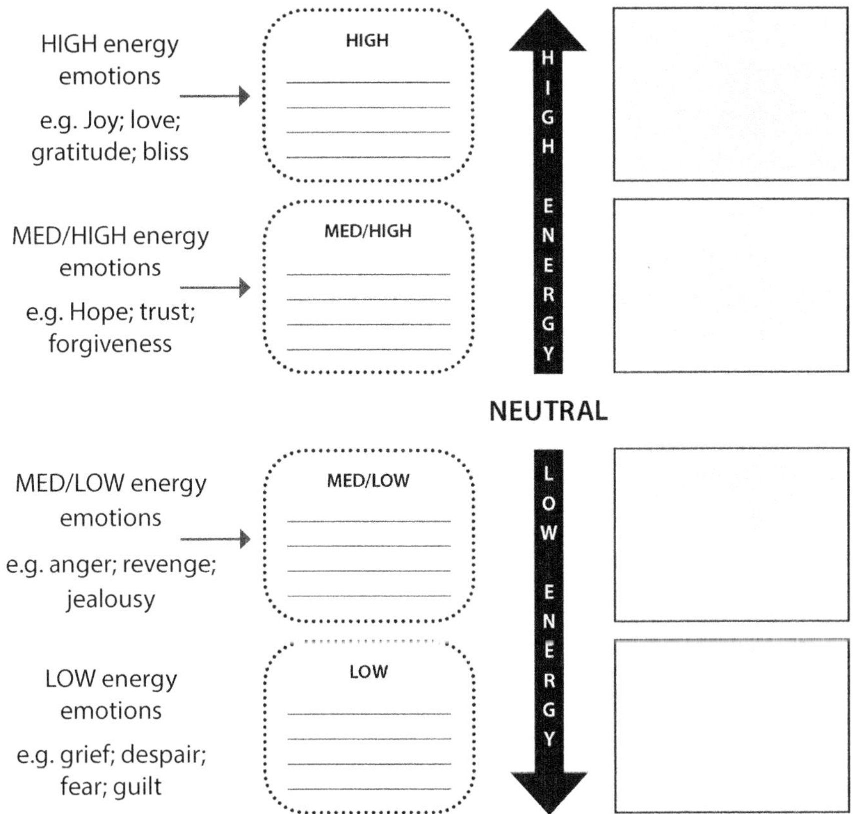

Higher Energy Emotions

ACCEPTANCE: Release the need to control and make peace with change.

AMAZEMENT: Overwhelmed with astonishment.

CONFIDENCE: Having faith in yourself and your abilities.

DETERMINATION: A clear intention set on achieving something.

EMPATHY: To identify with another's feelings as if they were your own.

EXCITEMENT: Feeling energised and motivated to act.

FEARLESSNESS: Not being daunted by challenges, intimidation or worries.

FREEDOM: Liberated, self-determined, autonomy, a feeling of independence.

FORGIVENESS: The release of negative emotions towards another who has wronged you.

GRATITUDE: Thankfulness, appreciation for what is.

HAPPINESS: Joyful contentment.

HOPEFULNESS: Optimistic, looking forward positive outlook.

INSPIRATION: Feeling motivated to do something positive.

LOVE: A deep affection and connection to someone or something.

OPTIMISM: Hope, confidence and positivity for what is to come.

PASSION: Enthusiastic, motivated and driven to do something.

PEACEFULNESS: Experiencing a state of complete calm and serenity.

POSITIVITY: Optimistic, hopeful and upbeat about the future.

RELIEF: A lighter feeling that comes from releasing stressors.

SATISFACTION: Feeling content and fulfilled.

TRUST: Having faith and confidence.

VALUED: Feeling worthy and appreciated.

VINDICATED: Set free from guilt being proven right.

WONDERMENT: Feeling awe and amazement.

Lower Energy Emotions

ANGER: Strong feelings of displeasure often associated with a sense of injustice.

ANXIETY: Intense feelings of worry sometimes for no reason.

BITTERNESS: Deep unhappiness that occurs when you feel you've been wronged.

DEPRESSION: In a state of withdrawal and sadness; low energy.

DESIRE: a yearning related to someone or something you want or don't want.

DESPAIR: A lack of hope.

DISAPPOINTMENT: Feeling let down.

EMBARRASSMENT: Self-conscious discomfort.

ENVY: To be resentful of someone else's good fortune.

GRIEF: Deep rooted sorrow relating to personal loss.

GUILT: Feeling a sense of blame for something.

HUMILIATON: Feeling degraded or worthless.

JEALOUSY: Anger towards another for a perceived advantage they have.

LONELINESS: Feeling isolated or cut off from others emotionally and/or physically.

NEGLECT: Feeling ignored, unloved, side-lined by another.

OVERWHELM: Feeling overcome/overpowered emotionally and/or physically.

POWERLESSNESS: Feeling overwhelmed; unable to take control.

REGRET: Sadness resulting from something that cannot be changed.

REVENGE: Wanting to get your own back on someone who has wronged you.

SADNESS: Feeling unhappy, sorrowful, depressed and in despair.

SELF-LOATHING: Intense dislike or hatred of oneself.

SELF-PITY: Feeling sorry for yourself, self-indulgent rumination over problems.

SHAME: Feeling disgraced for acting improperly even if not to blame.

WORTHLESSNESS: Feelings of insignificance and not being valued.

3. Categorise by Mindset and/or Activity

   Finally, use the four boxes to the right of the arrows to divide the list into either:

   - MINDSET (see Sample Chart #1 on page 16), or
   - ACTIVITY (see Sample Chart #2 on page 17).

   In each instance, think of a word that:

   - Describes your MINDSET when you're experiencing these emotions, or
   - Describes the ACTIVITY you do when you're in a specific emotional state.

   TIP: You can either create two separate charts divided into mindset and activity or combine them into one chart as outlined on page 15.

Why this works

MINDSET: Dividing emotions into MINDSET categories will help you recognise what you're thinking when you experience particular emotions. Doing this will make you more aware of the beliefs driving your mindset. This helps you get a better understanding of the belief systems subconsciously driving your emotional responses to what's going on in your life.

ACTIVITIES: Dividing your emotions into ACTIVITY categories helps you recognise how you behave when you're experiencing certain emotional states. This is a useful tool for identifying helpful and unhelpful behaviours and recognise activities that could pull you up the emotional scale. For example, even though you know going for a walk will raise your mood, you might not feel like doing it. But recognising the positive impact of going for walk can help you do it, despite not wanting to. Knowing what helps you feel better can motivate you to do it, rather than just thinking about it.

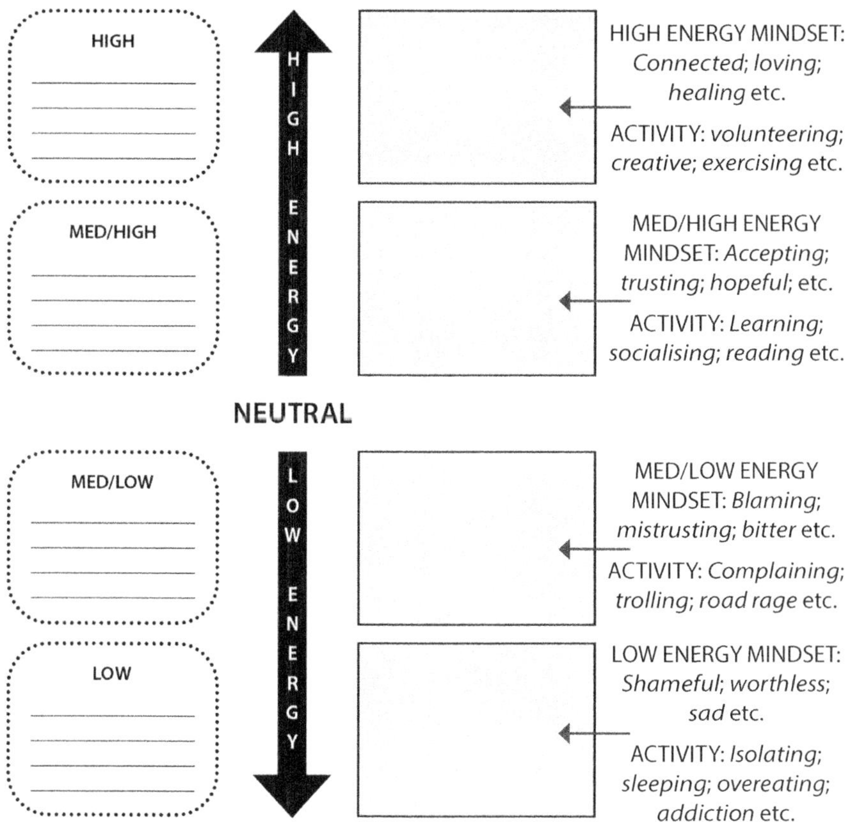
HIGH
MED/HIGH
MED/LOW
LOW
HIGH ENERGY
NEUTRAL
LOW ENERGY
HIGH ENERGY MINDSET: *Connected; loving; healing* etc.
ACTIVITY: *volunteering; creative; exercising* etc.
MED/HIGH ENERGY MINDSET: *Accepting; trusting; hopeful;* etc.
ACTIVITY: *Learning; socialising; reading* etc.
MED/LOW ENERGY MINDSET: *Blaming; mistrusting; bitter* etc.
ACTIVITY: *Complaining; trolling; road rage* etc.
LOW ENERGY MINDSET: *Shameful; worthless; sad* etc.
ACTIVITY: *Isolating; sleeping; overeating; addiction* etc.

EXAMPLE OF A COMPLETED EMOTIONAL SCALE CHART #1: MINDSET

HIGH ENERGY

HIGH
Joy
Love
Peace
Gratitude

HIGH ENERGY MINDSET: UNITY
'I feel connected to everything and love my life.'

MED/HIGH
Forgiveness
Enthusiasm
Hope
Trust

MED/HIGH ENERGY MINDSET: ACCEPT
'I accept where I am and trust it will work out.'

NEUTRAL

LOW ENERGY

MED/LOW
Arrogance
Anger
Revenge
Envy

MED/LOW ENERGY MINDSET: BLAME
'Everything is someone else's fault.'

LOW
Anxiety
Grief
Despair
Guilt

LOW ENERGY MINDSET: SHAME
'Everything is my fault. I'm not good enough.'

EXAMPLE OF A COMPLETED EMOTIONAL SCALE CHART #2: ACTIVITY

HIGH
Love
Peace
Gratitude
Freedom

HIGH ENERGY
Healthy eating
Meditating/Exercising
Volunteering
Connecting with nature

MED/HIGH
Forgiveness
Positivity
Optimism
Trust

MED/HIGH ENERGY
Learning new things
Socialising
Setting goals
Letting go of the past

HIGH ENERGY

NEUTRAL

LOW ENERGY

MED/LOW
Anger
Revenge
Jealousy
Desire

MED/LOW ENERGY
Complaining
Excessive social media
Arguing
Lack of empathy

LOW
Sadness
Grief
Worthlessness
Guilt

LOW ENERGY
Sleeping
Isolating
Addictive behaviours
Procrastinating

EMOTIONAL SCALE CHART

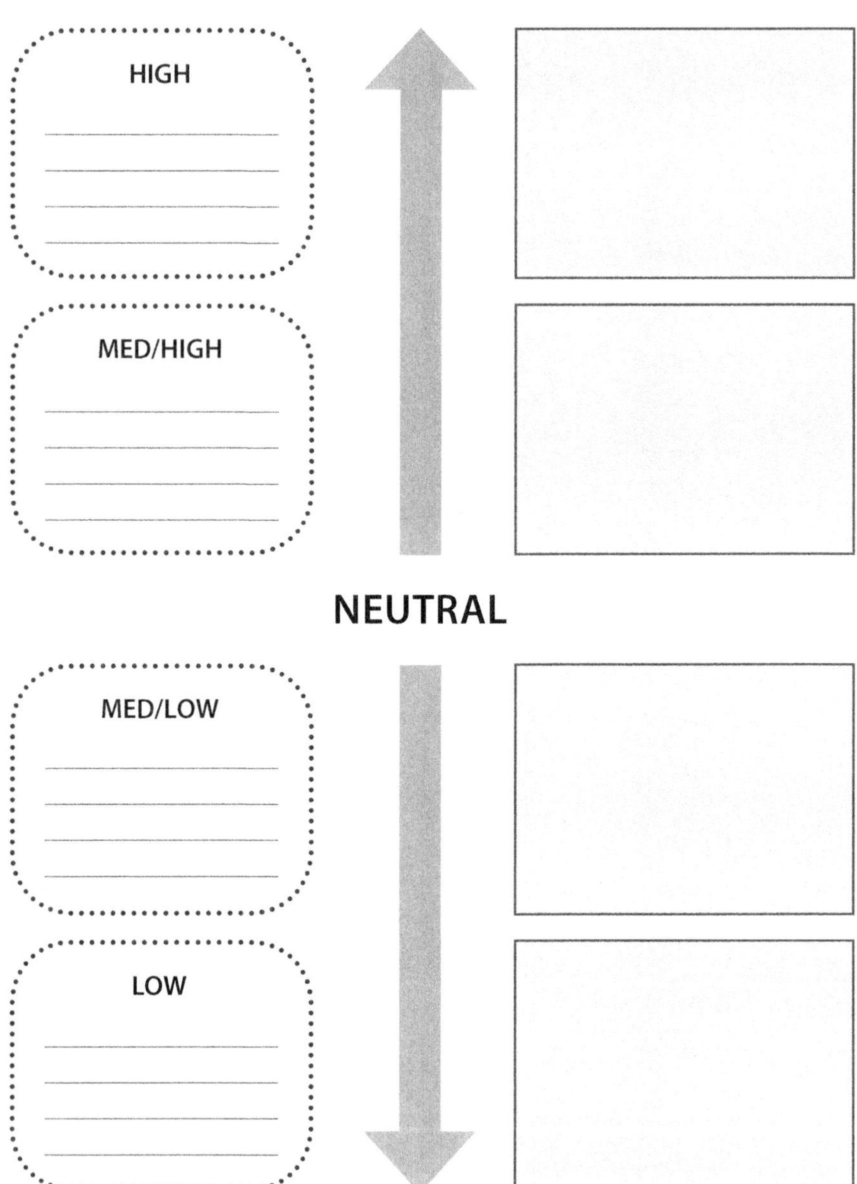

EMOTIONAL SCALE CHART

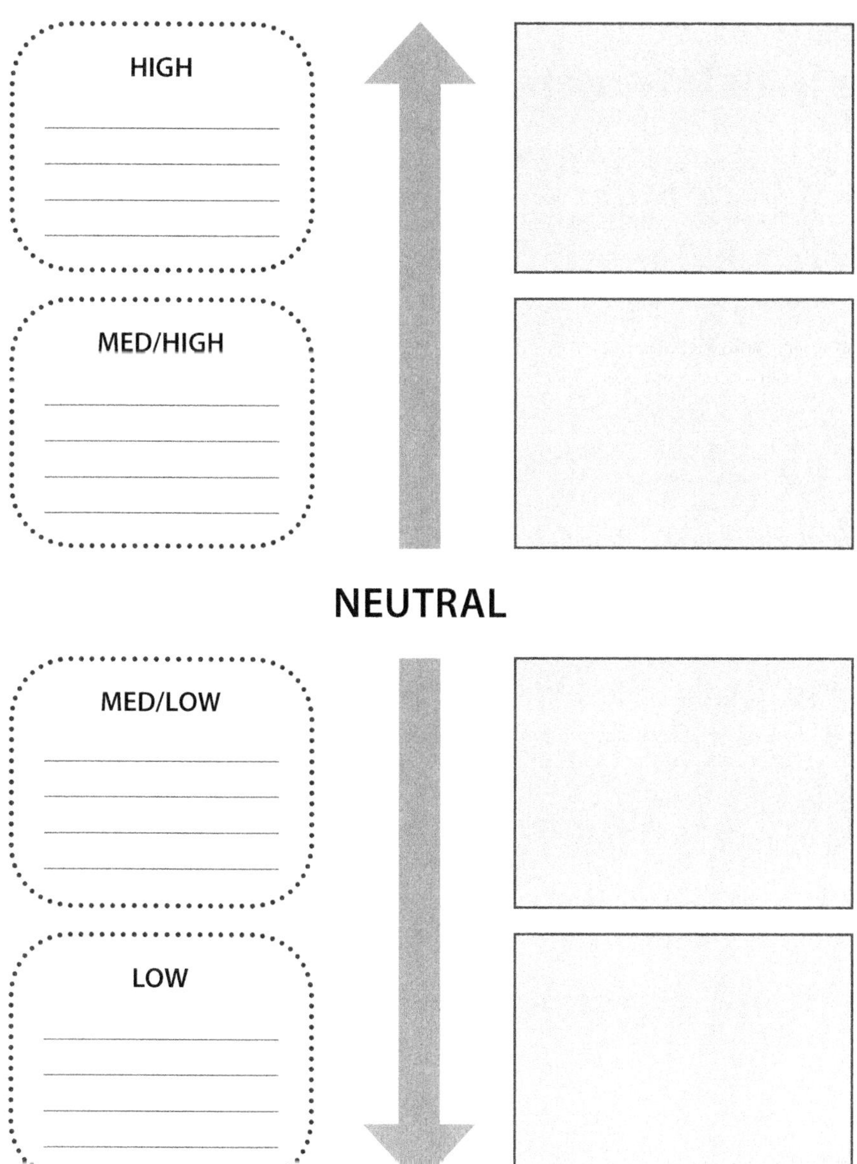

EMOTIONAL SCALE CHART

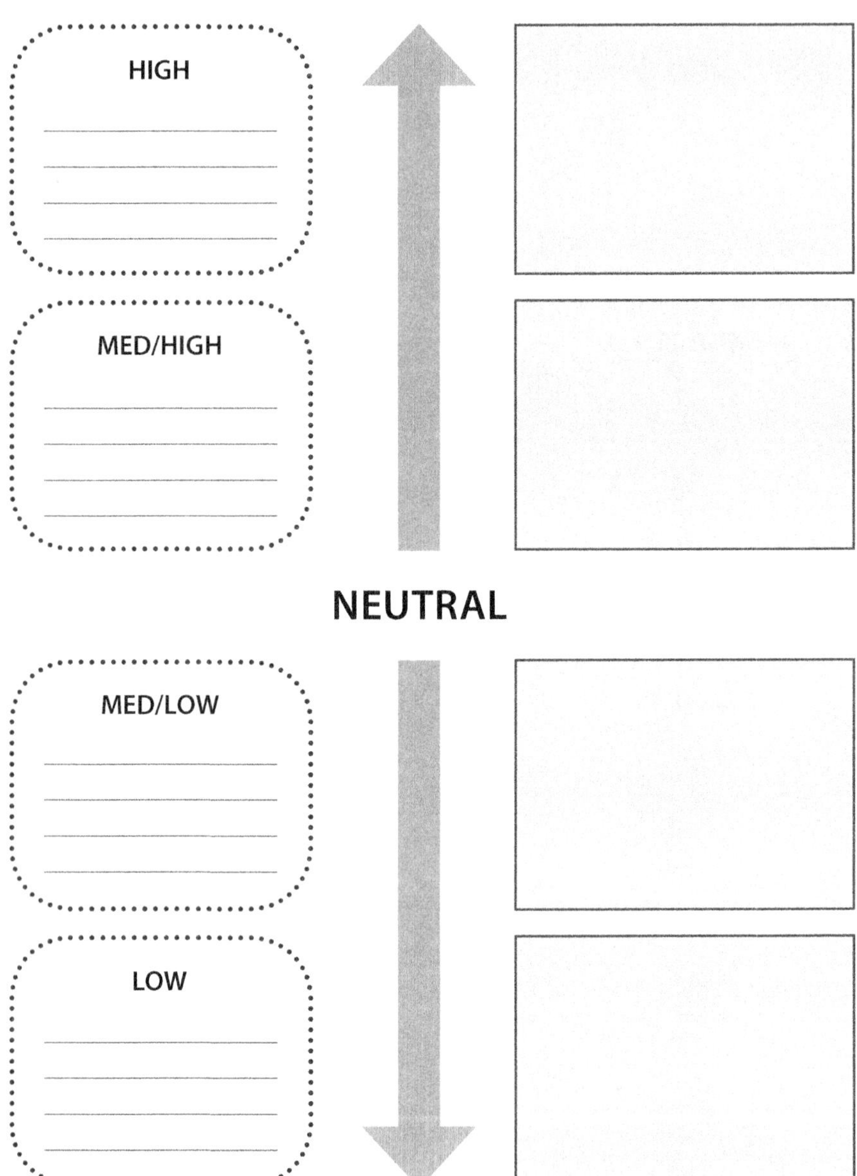

EMOTIONAL SCALE CHART

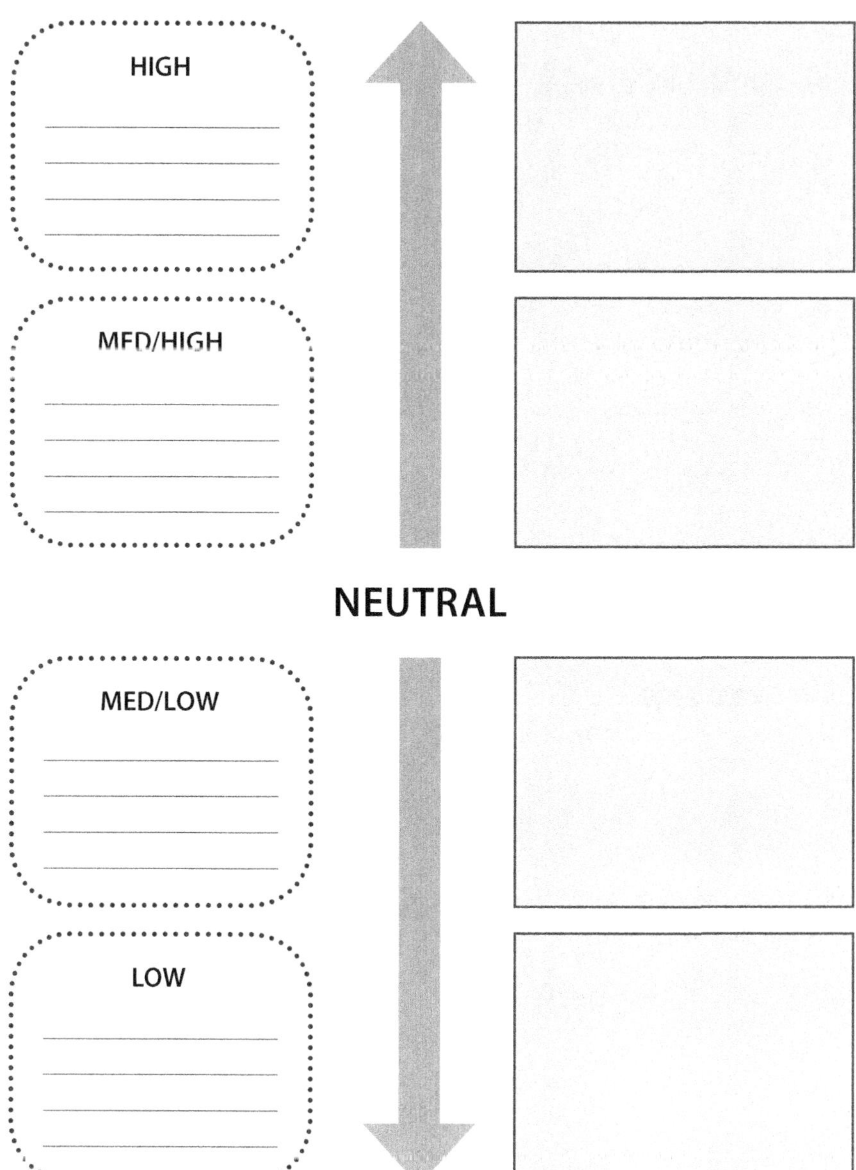

EMOTIONAL SCALE CHART

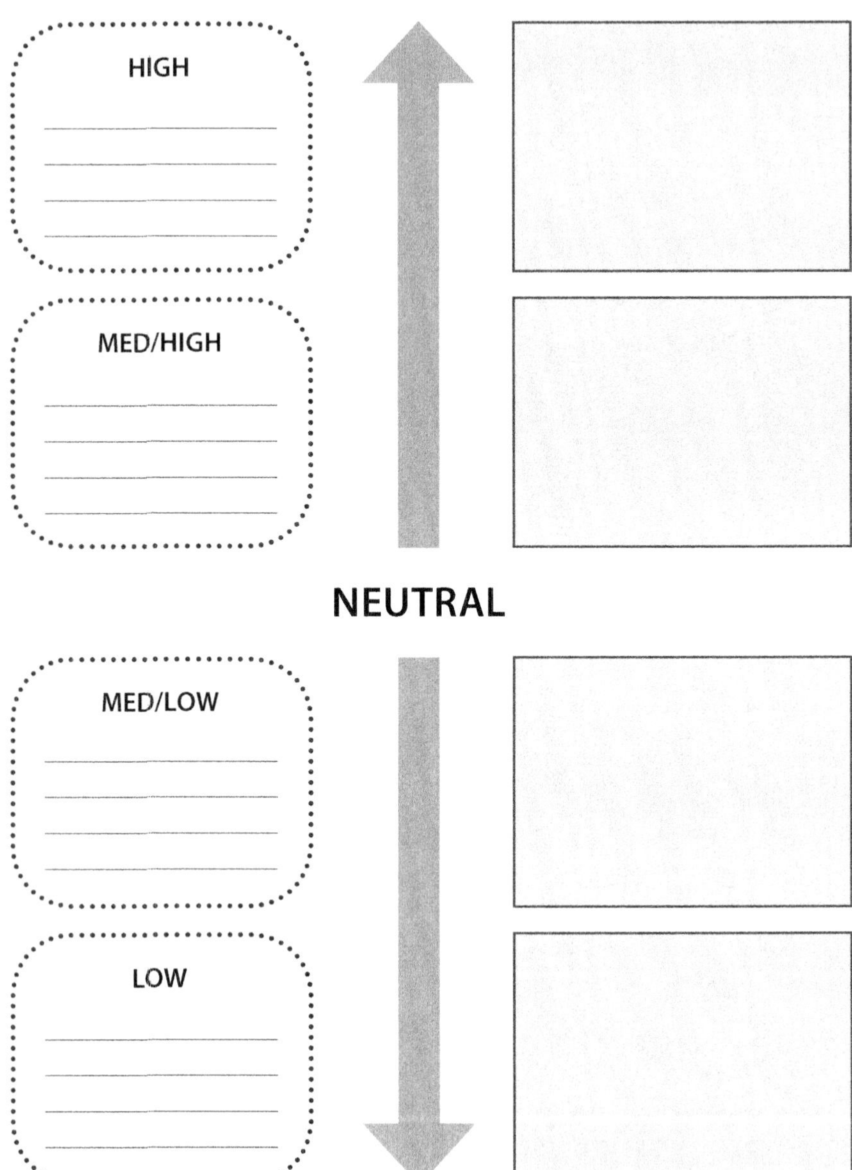

EMOTIONAL SCALE CHART

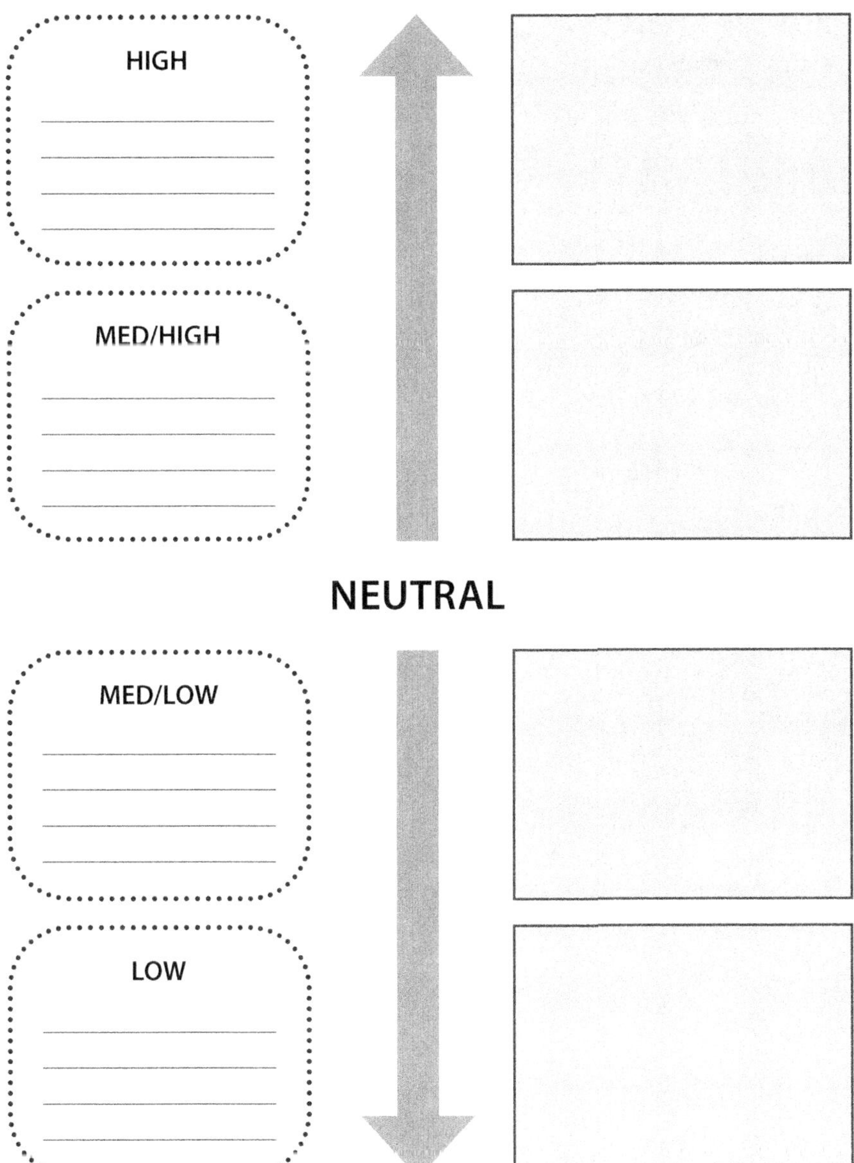

EMOTIONAL SCALE CHART

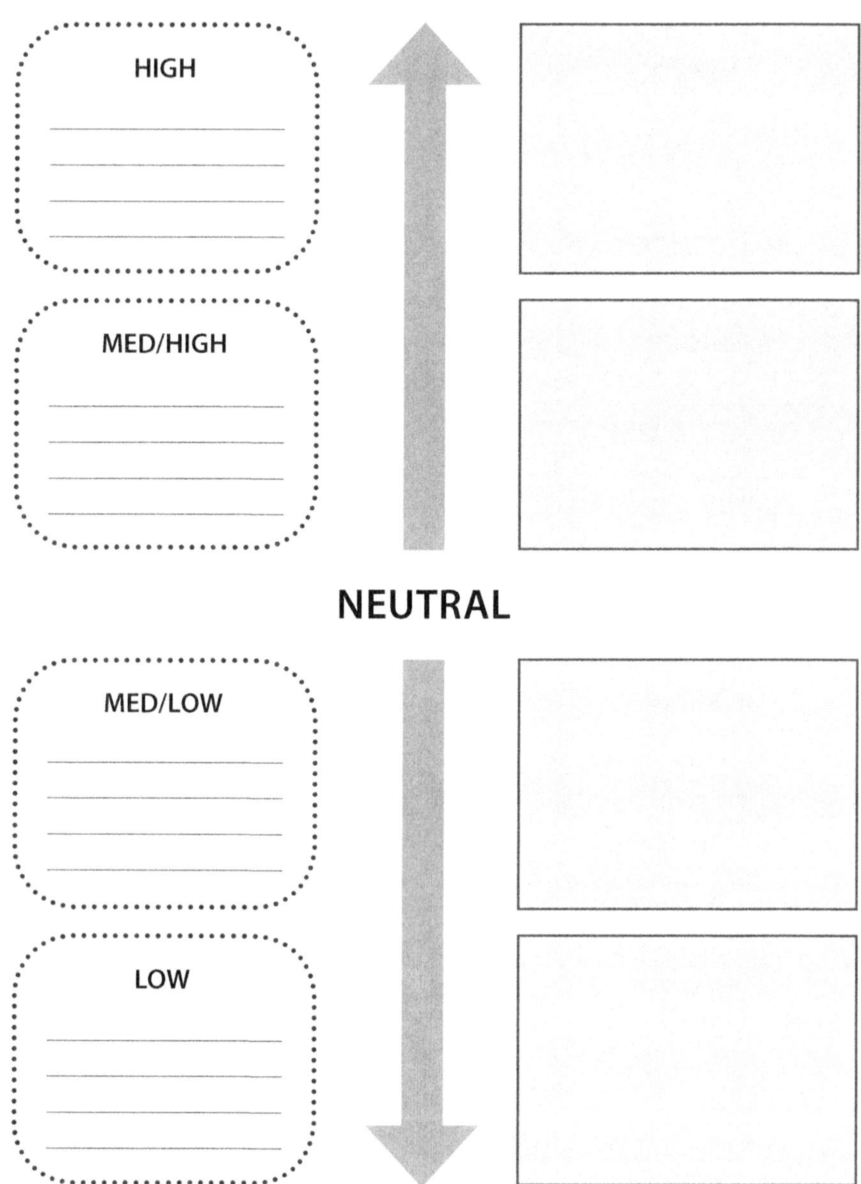

EMOTIONAL SCALE CHART

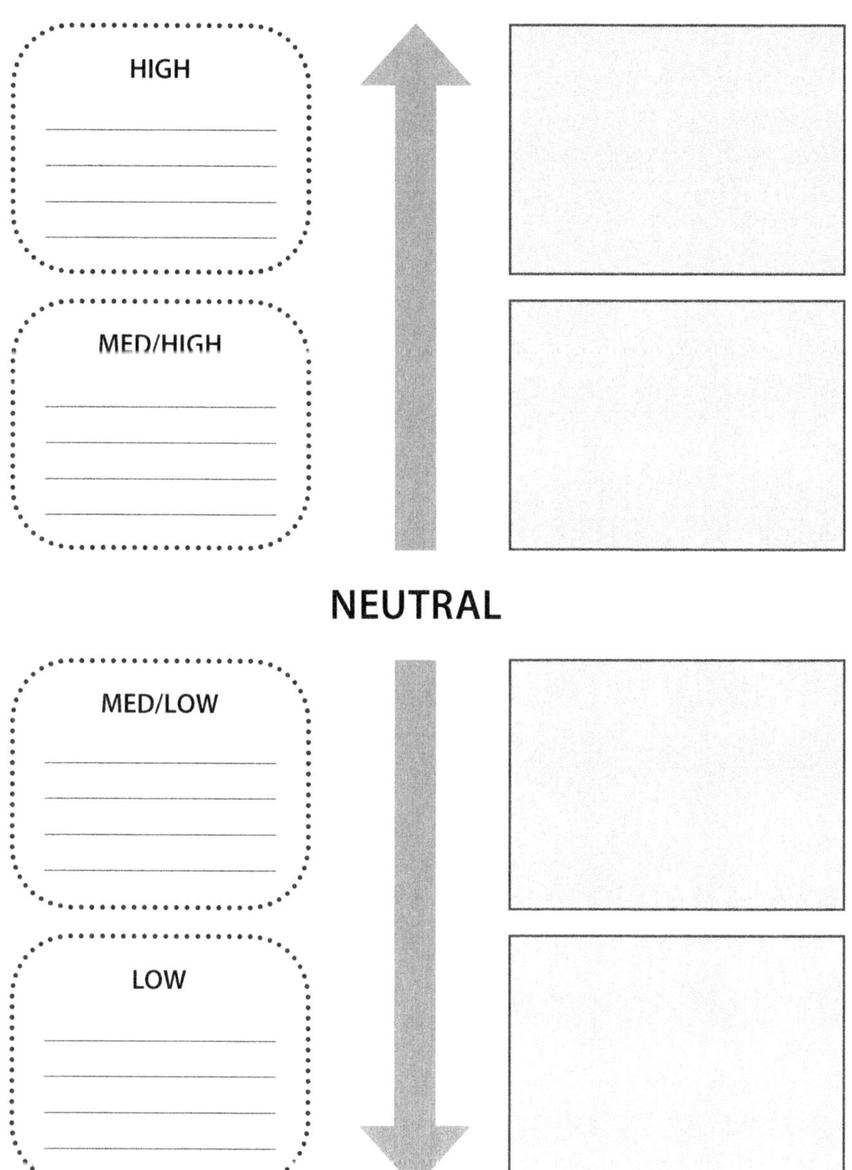

EMOTIONAL SCALE CHART

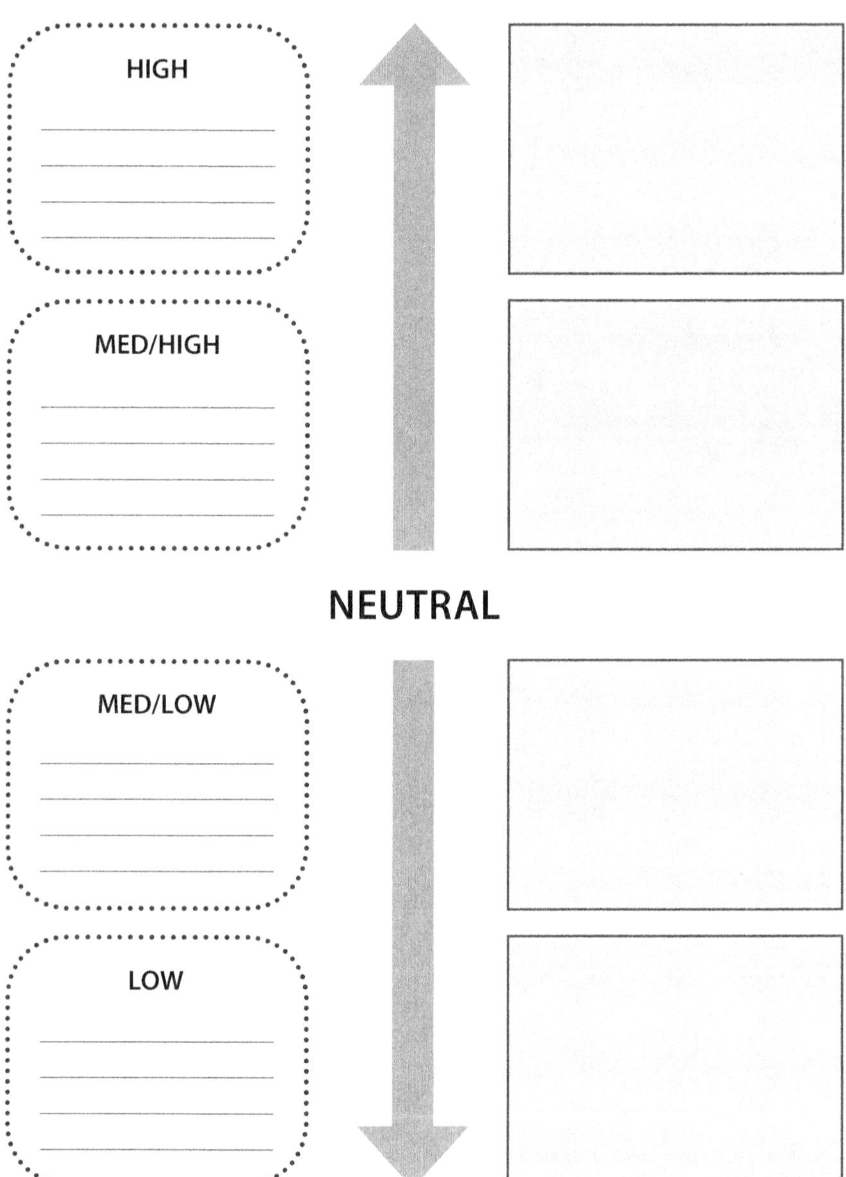

EMOTIONAL SCALE CHART

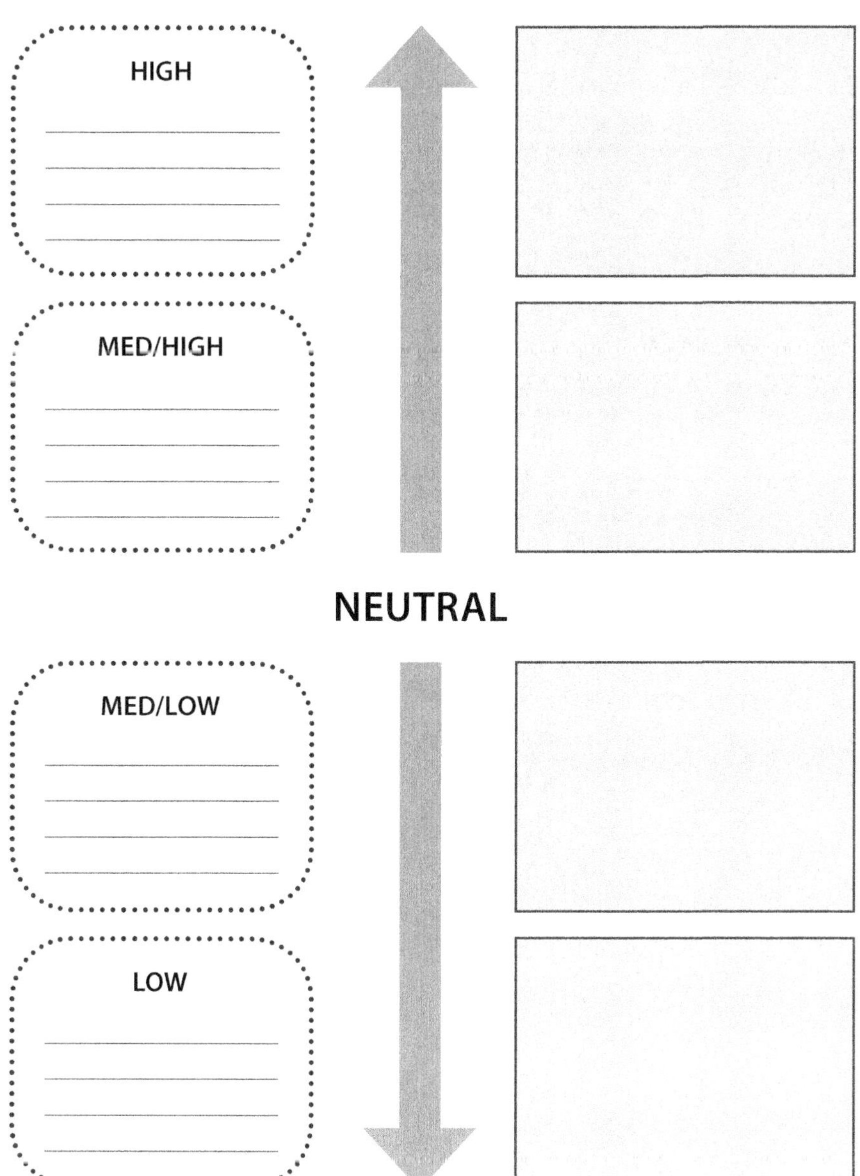

EMOTIONAL SCALE CHART

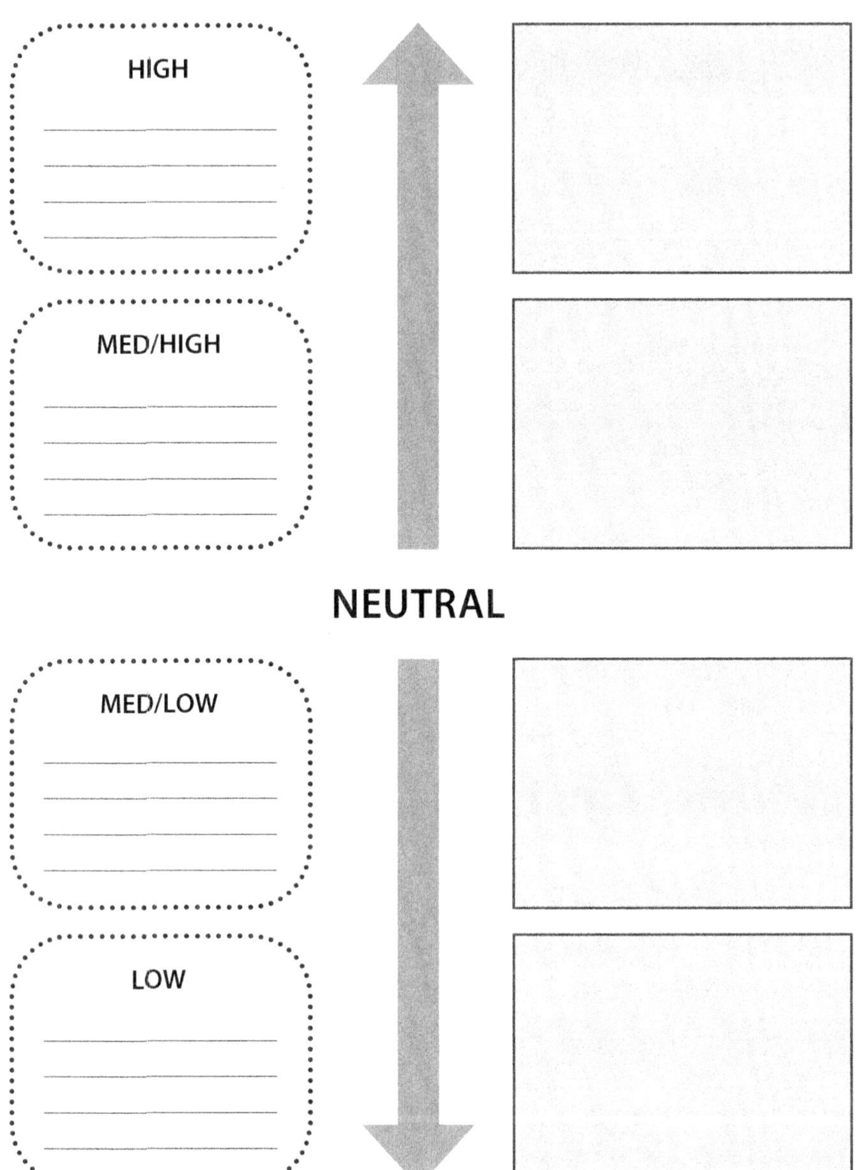

EMOTIONAL SCALE CHART

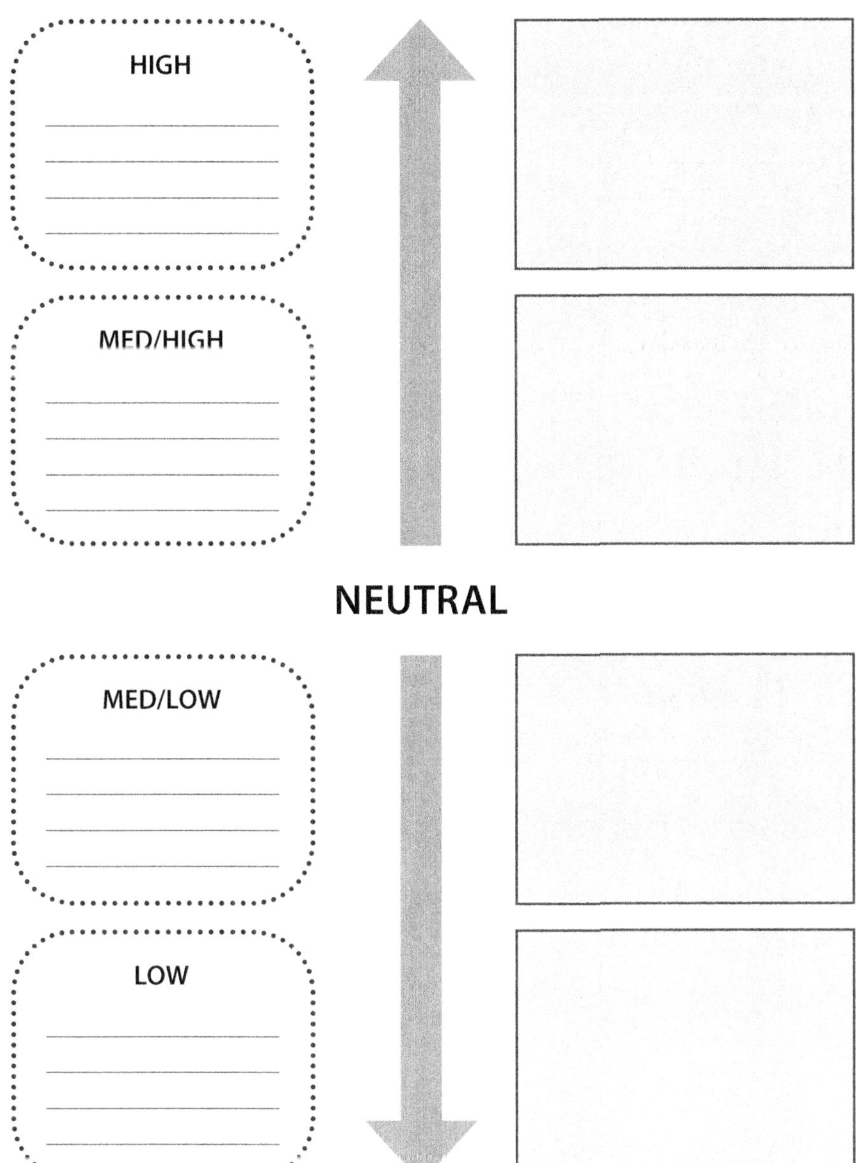

EMOTIONAL SCALE CHART

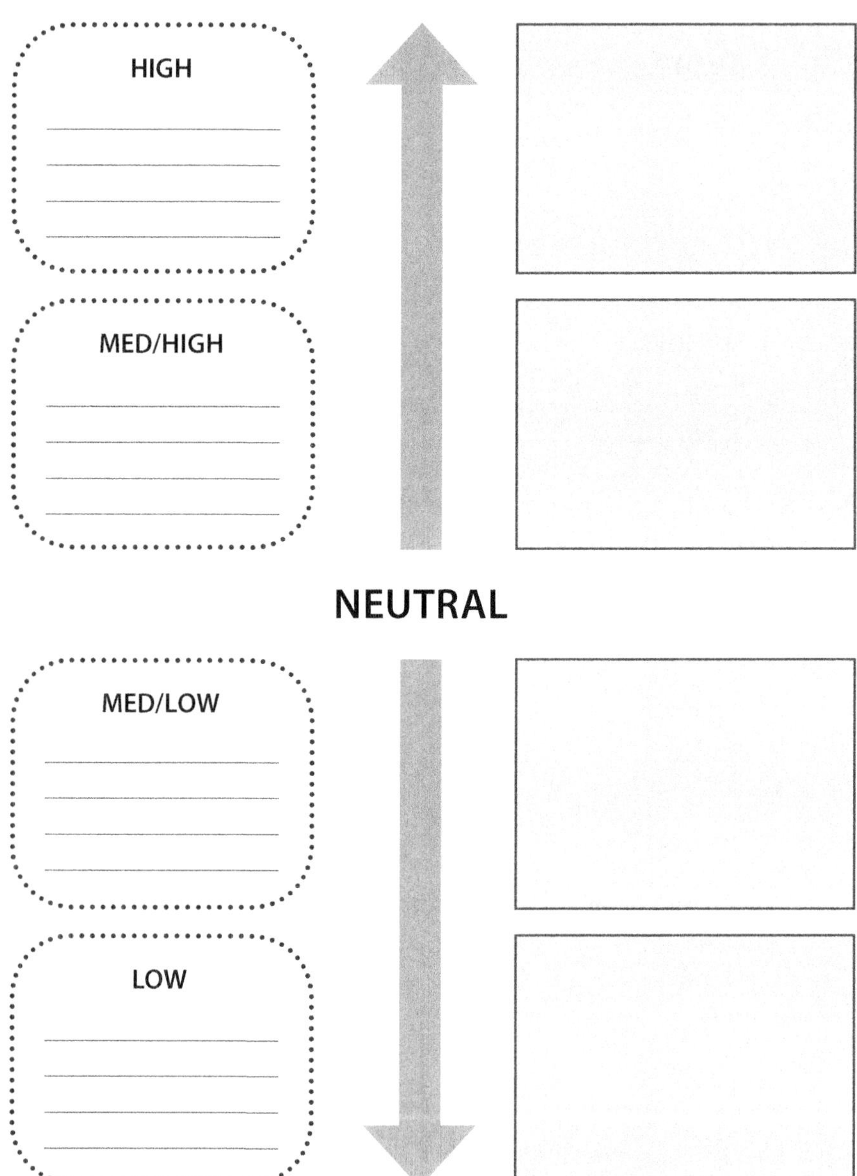

EMOTIONAL SCALE CHART

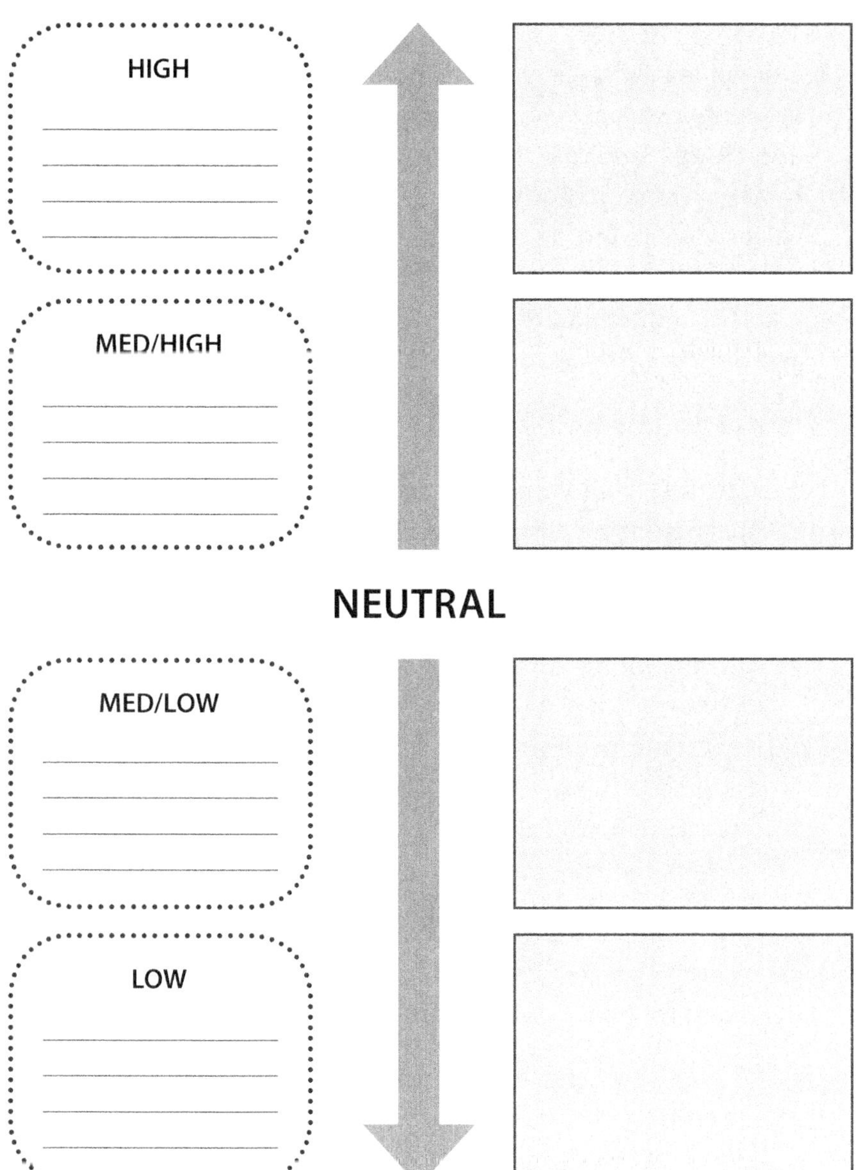

2. Values List

What are values?

Our values indicate what is important to us. They can include emotional states, such as peace, love and joy as well as people and things in our life that give us high-energy feelings. You can have values around any area of your life, including your health, wealth, wellbeing, family, career and much more. Your values reflect what's important to you in your life right now. Some values are constant while others change depending on your situation and different periods of your life.

How to create a values category list

- Use the Values Word List on page 33 to find words (and values) that resonate with you. There is space to add your own if you want to. Feel free to highlight ones that resonate, reflecting a positive emotional response.
- Use the tables on pages 35–39 to organise your values into different categories e.g. health; work, finances, relationships, personal development, mental health, wellbeing etc. You can divide them further if you wish, e.g. values for a specific relationship or health goal or for a specific period of your life. See example on page 34

TIP: If you notice the same values coming up in all the different categories, it can indicate that they're core values for you, so you may want to use them in your daily list.

VALUES WORD LIST

Acceptance	Achievement	Assertiveness	Awareness
Balance	Beauty	Bravery	Calm
Challenge	Charity	Commitment	Communication
Community	Compassion	Connection	Creativity
Dedication	Determination	Development	Discipline
Discovery	Empathy	Empowerment	Endurance
Energy	Enjoyment	Enthusiasm	Equality
Experience	Exploration	Fairness	Family
Fame	Feelings	Fidelity	Focus
Freedom	Friendship	Fun	Giving
Gratitude	Growth	Happiness	Hard work
Harmony	Health	Honesty	Hope
Humour	Imagination	Independence	Individuality
Inspiration	Integrity	Intuition	Joy
Justice	Kindness	Knowledge	Logic
Love	Loyalty	Motivation	Optimism
Order	Passion	Patience	Peace
Pets	Power	Presence	Prosperity
Purpose	Recognition	Recreation	Respect
Responsibility	Security	Sincerity	Solitude
Spirituality	Support	Trust	Truth
Unity	Vision	Vitality	Wealth

Add any words of your own in the space below.

EXAMPLE OF A VALUES CATEGORY LIST

Values for: Work			
Achievement	Assertiveness	Balance	Challenge
Commitment	Dedication	Determination	Development
Enjoyment	Experience	Focus	Growth
Knowledge	Loyalty	Motivation	Prosperity
Recognition	Respect	Responsibility	Support

Values for: Working on a relationship			
Acceptance	Awareness	Commitment	Communication
Compassion	Connection	Dedication	Empathy
Equality	Family	Fidelity	Friendship
Fun	Harmony	Honesty	Humour
Independence	Love	Loyalty	Passion

Values for: Wealth creation			
Abundance	Challenge	Creativity	Determination
Discovery	Empowerment	Endurance	Exploration
Focus	Freedom	Growth	Hope
Inspiration	Intuition	Investment	Knowledge
Purpose	Security	Vision	Wealth

Values for: To improve health			
Balance	Calm	Communication	Compassion
Discovery	Empowerment	Energy	Enjoyment
Exploration	Focus	Gratitude	Growth
Harmony	Health	Knowledge	Motivation
Patience	Peace	Pets	Purpose
Solitude	Support	Vision	Vitality

VALUES CATEGORY TEMPLATES

Values for:			

Values for:			

Values for:			

Values for:			

VALUES CATEGORY TEMPLATES

Values for:			

Values for:			

Values for:			

Values for:			

VALUES CATEGORY TEMPLATES

Values for:			

Values for:			

Values for:			

Values for:			

VALUES CATEGORY TEMPLATES

Values for:			

Values for:			

Values for:			

Values for:			

VALUES CATEGORY TEMPLATES

Values for:			

Values for:			

Values for:			

Values for:			

How to create and use your daily values list

Now that you have your values divided into categories, you can start selecting the ones you want to focus on as part of your daily practice. This is where your daily values list comes in.

You can write out a new list of values every day or write one and keep using it over a period of time. If you want to focus on achieving one specific outcome, stick to one category but if not, you can create a more general list.

Use the blank templates provided in this book or use your own journal to write out your values. Alternatively, jot them down on a sticky note and put them somewhere you can see them throughout the day. You could even type your values into your phone, so you can read them when you're on the go.

- Choose up to six values each day from any category you like. Aim for words that give you a sense of love, joy and purpose when you read them.
- Spend a little time focusing on each of these values and consider why they are so important to you. You should notice a shift in your energy as your attention moves away from what causes you stress and towards what brings you joy.

TIP: You don't need to create a new list of values every day, you can keep using the same one until you are ready to create a new one or it becomes less relevant to what you want to focus on.

Why this works

Where you place your attention is where your energy goes, which is why you need to consciously choose what to focus on each day. By deciding which values to live by, you ensure your energy goes into what you want in your life, not what you don't want. It helps raise your emotional level at the start of the day enabling you to break unhelpful thinking habits and live more intentionally.

DAILY VALUES LISTS

DAILY VALUES LIST
1
2
3
4
5
6

DAILY VALUES LIST
1
2
3
4
5
6

DAILY VALUES LIST
1
2
3
4
5
6

DAILY VALUES LIST
1
2
3
4
5
6

DAILY VALUES LIST
1
2
3
4
5
6

DAILY VALUES LIST
1
2
3
4
5
6

DAILY VALUES LIST
1
2
3
4
5
6

DAILY VALUES LIST
1
2
3
4
5
6

DAILY VALUES LISTS

DAILY VALUES LIST
1
2
3
4
5
6

DAILY VALUES LIST
1
2
3
4
5
6

DAILY VALUES LIST
1
2
3
4
5
6

DAILY VALUES LIST
1
2
3
4
5
6

DAILY VALUES LIST
1
2
3
4
5
6

DAILY VALUES LIST
1
2
3
4
5
6

DAILY VALUES LIST
1
2
3
4
5
6

DAILY VALUES LIST
1
2
3
4
5
6

DAILY VALUES LISTS

DAILY VALUES LIST
1
2
3
4
5
6

DAILY VALUES LIST
1
2
3
4
5
6

DAILY VALUES LIST
1
2
3
4
5
6

DAILY VALUES LIST
1
2
3
4
5
6

DAILY VALUES LIST
1
2
3
4
5
6

DAILY VALUES LIST
1
2
3
4
5
6

DAILY VALUES LIST
1
2
3
4
5
6

DAILY VALUES LIST
1
2
3
4
5
6

DAILY VALUES LISTS

DAILY VALUES LIST
1
2
3
4
5
6

DAILY VALUES LIST
1
2
3
4
5
6

DAILY VALUES LIST
1
2
3
4
5
6

DAILY VALUES LIST
1
2
3
4
5
6

DAILY VALUES LIST
1
2
3
4
5
6

DAILY VALUES LIST
1
2
3
4
5
6

DAILY VALUES LIST
1
2
3
4
5
6

DAILY VALUES LIST
1
2
3
4
5
6

DAILY VALUES LISTS

DAILY VALUES LIST
1
2
3
4
5
6

DAILY VALUES LIST
1
2
3
4
5
6

DAILY VALUES LIST
1
2
3
4
5
6

DAILY VALUES LIST
1
2
3
4
5
6

DAILY VALUES LIST
1
2
3
4
5
6

DAILY VALUES LIST
1
2
3
4
5
6

DAILY VALUES LIST
1
2
3
4
5
6

DAILY VALUES LIST
1
2
3
4
5
6

DAILY VALUES LISTS

DAILY VALUES LIST
1
2
3
4
5
6

DAILY VALUES LIST
1
2
3
4
5
6

DAILY VALUES LIST
1
2
3
4
5
6

DAILY VALUES LIST
1
2
3
4
5
6

DAILY VALUES LIST
1
2
3
4
5
6

DAILY VALUES LIST
1
2
3
4
5
6

DAILY VALUES LIST
1
2
3
4
5
6

DAILY VALUES LIST
1
2
3
4
5
6

DAILY VALUES LISTS

DAILY VALUES LIST
1
2
3
4
5
6

DAILY VALUES LIST
1
2
3
4
5
6

DAILY VALUES LIST
1
2
3
4
5
6

DAILY VALUES LIST
1
2
3
4
5
6

DAILY VALUES LIST
1
2
3
4
5
6

DAILY VALUES LIST
1
2
3
4
5
6

DAILY VALUES LIST
1
2
3
4
5
6

DAILY VALUES LIST
1
2
3
4
5
6

DAILY VALUES LISTS

DAILY VALUES LIST
1
2
3
4
5
6

DAILY VALUES LIST
1
2
3
4
5
6

DAILY VALUES LIST
1
2
3
4
5
6

DAILY VALUES LIST
1
2
3
4
5
6

DAILY VALUES LIST
1
2
3
4
5
6

DAILY VALUES LIST
1
2
3
4
5
6

DAILY VALUES LIST
1
2
3
4
5
6

DAILY VALUES LIST
1
2
3
4
5
6

3. Affirmations

An affirmation is simply a written statement designed to help you focus on what you want. The idea with all affirmations is that you repeat them a number of times as you go through the day. By doing this, your subconscious gradually accepts them as true.

How to write affirmations

Use the blank templates provided on pages 52–57.

- Begin by deciding which categories you want to create affirmations for, e.g. work, relationships, health, money, etc.
- Write out your affirmations focusing on what you want, rather than what you don't, e.g. writing about getting out of debt will have you focus on the debt, not the abundance you want to create; writing an affirmation on getting rid of a particular health condition will have you focus on the condition rather than your health.
- Pick the affirmation you want to focus on and repeat it often during the day, either out loud or in your head, until you start to accept it on a subconscious level. Alternatively, write it out and put it where you'll see it throughout the day so you read and think about it.

Affirmation writing tips

- Use the present tense: Write the statement as if it has already happened, e.g. 'I am abundant' rather than the future 'I will be abundant.' This makes the affirmation more effective as you start to believe it to be true.
- Avoid certain words: Avoid words like 'but', 'try', 'must' and 'should', which make it seem like you're obliged to do something, for example, 'I must try to work harder to become successful'. Instead, try a more positive statement such as 'I am successful and enjoy my work'.

- Stay in touch with your emotions: If the affirmation doesn't resonate with you, it may not be the right one. Also, if you make it too unbelievable you won't resonate with it. Keep it positive but realistic.
- Start with gratitude: Gratitude will always lift your mood as it proves you have something to be grateful for. So, try adding 'I am thankful for…' at the start of your affirmation and see how it makes you feel.

Why this works

We often have ideas and beliefs that are so deeply ingrained in our subconscious that we're not even aware they exist. Affirmations help us switch our focus to what we want to create in our lives, so the more we repeat them the more we can integrate them into our thinking. That makes it easier to start replacing unhelpful beliefs and thought patterns with more beneficial ones.

EXAMPLES OF AFFIRMATIONS

Affirmations for work

- "I am focused on my goals and feel passionate about my work."
- "I balance my career and personal life so both are in harmony."
- "Success comes to me through the right opportunities."

Affirmations for love and relationships

- "The more I love myself, the more love I receive from others."
- "I only attract people who treat me with love and respect."
- "I develop loving relationships easily."

Affirmations for wealth and abundance

- "Wealth and abundance come to me in both expected and unexpected ways."
- "I am grateful to be able to create money whenever I want it."
- "I easily create money and abundance."

Affirmations for health

- "The older I get, the healthier I become."
- "I lovingly do all I can to keep my body in perfect health."
- "My body heals quickly and easily."

Affirmations for acceptance

- "I love and accept where I am right now."
- "I know and accept that things are always working out for me."
- "I am open to all opportunities for positive change today."

Affirmations for forgiveness

- "I am grateful for the inner peace that forgiveness brings me."
- "I let go of the past with love and embrace the future with excitement."
- "Forgiveness is a gift to myself."

Affirmations for self-love

- "I am enough."
- "My life is a gift and I am worthy of love and joy."
- "I am creating my life, exactly as I want it."

AFFIRMATION LISTS

Affirmations for: ____________________

AFFIRMATION LISTS

Affirmations for: ________________________________

AFFIRMATION LISTS

Affirmations for: ______________________________

AFFIRMATION LISTS

Affirmations for: ______________________________

AFFIRMATION LISTS

Affirmations for: ______________________________

AFFIRMATION LISTS

Affirmations for: ______________________________

4. Stress Diary

If you want to live more mindfully, it's helpful to start noticing what triggers stress in your life. You might be tempted only to consider major stress events, but what you might not realise is that it's often the smaller daily stressors – the micro-stressors – that trigger the most stress. The lists below give examples of both major and minor sources of stress.

Examples of major stress events	Examples of minor stress events
Illness	Driving
Bereavement	Negativity from others
Changes at work	Work/life imbalance
Promotion	Money worries
Divorce	Environmental stress: mess/noise
Marriage	Negative self-talk
House move	Digital stress: social media/emails

How to keep a stress diary

Keep a diary logging stressful events to help you become aware of your personal stress triggers (see the examples on page 59). Use the sample stress diary on page 61 as a guide and follow the instructions given with it.

You can either keep a stress diary for a period of a week so you get an idea of when you get most stressed or you could just use it as a one-off exercise when you experience higher levels of stress.

Why this works

Noticing the level of stress you're experiencing will raise your awareness of any patterns and regular triggers in your life, making it easier for you to look out for and prepare for them. You may notice there are certain times of the day when your mood is lower and your feelings of stress higher than others. Once you're aware of what factors trigger you to feel stressed, you can use mindfulness to let go of any thoughts associated with those triggers and choose better responses.

TIP: Some find keeping a stress diary a useful way to start getting a better understanding of themselves, but for others it can become a burden. If that's the case for you, just stop otherwise it will end up being counter-productive.

EXAMPLE OF A COMPLETED STRESS DIARY

DATE: 12/4/22

TIME	MOOD SCALE 0-10	STRESS LEVEL 0-10	WHAT CAUSED STRESS?	HOW DID YOU MANAGE IT? 0-10
7.30 am	8	5	Alarm didn't go off	8 - stayed quite calm
8.30 am	6	8	Stuck in traffic	2 - got mad with other drivers
10.15 am	5	8	Annoying work colleague wound me up!	8 - did breathwork felt OK!
5.30 pm	7	4	Stuck in traffic again!	8 - took my time, enjoyed the drive.
7.15 pm	4	8	Kids were arguing!	2 - shouted at them.

Stress diary exercise

If you fill out the following pages as set out in the sample stress diary, you'll start to notice your stress triggers.

Mood scale – this indicates the mood you were in before the stressful event. This will help you see how your emotional state effects your response to stress, rather than just noticing the event itself.

- 0 = Low mood, e.g. tired/depressed.
- 10 = High mood, e.g. excited/optimistic.

Stress level – On a scale of 0-10, how stressed did you feel

- 0 = No stress
- 10 = High stress.

Stress management – How well did you deal with your stress?

- 0 = Not very well
- 10 = Very well

STRESS DIARY

DATE:

TIME	MOOD SCALE 0-10	STRESS LEVEL 0-10	WHAT CAUSED STRESS?	HOW DID YOU MANAGE IT? 0-10

STRESS DIARY

DATE:

TIME	MOOD SCALE 0-10	STRESS LEVEL 0-10	WHAT CAUSED STRESS?	HOW DID YOU MANAGE IT? 0-10

STRESS DIARY

DATE:

TIME	MOOD SCALE 0-10	STRESS LEVEL 0-10	WHAT CAUSED STRESS?	HOW DID YOU MANAGE IT? 0-10

STRESS DIARY

DATE:

TIME	MOOD SCALE 0-10	STRESS LEVEL 0-10	WHAT CAUSED STRESS?	HOW DID YOU MANAGE IT? 0-10

STRESS DIARY

DATE:

TIME	MOOD SCALE 0-10	STRESS LEVEL 0-10	WHAT CAUSED STRESS?	HOW DID YOU MANAGE IT? 0-10

STRESS DIARY

DATE:

TIME	MOOD SCALE 0-10	STRESS LEVEL 0-10	WHAT CAUSED STRESS?	HOW DID YOU MANAGE IT? 0-10

STRESS DIARY

DATE:

TIME	MOOD SCALE 0-10	STRESS LEVEL 0-10	WHAT CAUSED STRESS?	HOW DID YOU MANAGE IT? 0-10

STRESS DIARY

DATE:

TIME	MOOD SCALE 0-10	STRESS LEVEL 0-10	WHAT CAUSED STRESS?	HOW DID YOU MANAGE IT? 0-10

STRESS DIARY

DATE:

TIME	MOOD SCALE 0-10	STRESS LEVEL 0-10	WHAT CAUSED STRESS?	HOW DID YOU MANAGE IT? 0-10

STRESS DIARY

DATE:

TIME	MOOD SCALE 0-10	STRESS LEVEL 0-10	WHAT CAUSED STRESS?	HOW DID YOU MANAGE IT? 0-10

STRESS DIARY

DATE:

TIME	MOOD SCALE 0-10	STRESS LEVEL 0-10	WHAT CAUSED STRESS?	HOW DID YOU MANAGE IT? 0-10

STRESS DIARY

DATE:

TIME	MOOD SCALE 0-10	STRESS LEVEL 0-10	WHAT CAUSED STRESS?	HOW DID YOU MANAGE IT? 0-10

STRESS DIARY

DATE:

TIME	MOOD SCALE 0-10	STRESS LEVEL 0-10	WHAT CAUSED STRESS?	HOW DID YOU MANAGE IT? 0-10

STRESS DIARY

DATE:

TIME	MOOD SCALE 0-10	STRESS LEVEL 0-10	WHAT CAUSED STRESS?	HOW DID YOU MANAGE IT? 0-10

HABIT FORMING EXERCISES

You may think it's big events that shape your life, because those are often what you remember, but if you think about it your day is made up of a chain of repeated habits. Many of these have been unconsciously ingrained into your routine for many years.

Mindfulness encourages you to start taking more notice of your daily habits by bringing them into conscious awareness. This puts you in a much better position for considering which habits are helpful (and worth keeping) and those that aren't and that you may want to stop. If you want to create new habits, you have to find ways to integrate them into your daily life on a conscious level until you get to a point where they too become habits. The following exercises are designed to help you develop habits that support your wellbeing and self-development practice.

5. Morning Reflection practice

Morning reflection is a quick and useful practice you can do daily to help you gain greater awareness of your regular thinking patterns.

How to do Morning Reflection practice

Use the blank templates on pages 77-86 to practice Morning Reflection.

- Each morning, make a quick note of your thoughts when you first wake up.
- Look for any patterns in your thinking and thoughts that come up repeatedly, for example relationship issues, money worries etc.
- Try adding a mindful reframe to this exercise by shifting your perspective, and notice if it has a positive impact on the way you feel (see examples on page 76).
- Repeat the exercise for 30 days or until you automatically become aware of your thoughts as you wake every day.

TIP: Don't dwell on your thoughts; simply notice them with interest, let them go and come back into the present. Make a note of whether they're linked to past events or are thoughts about the future.

Why this works

Noticing repetitive thoughts can give you greater insight into the belief systems that might be triggering them. You can then consider replacing these with different beliefs that create more beneficial and positive thoughts.

Morning Reflection practice – Example

Day 1

I woke up feeling anxious. I let go of thoughts to do with conflict at work and switched my focus to new opportunities that could arise. Felt better.

Day 2

Felt slightly depressed. Unhappy with health and weight. Shifted to recognising that change is possible and I don't have to do it all at once.

Day 3

Woke feeling stressed about money. Let it go as I know that worrying won't change things. Opening myself up to abundance. Let's see what happens! Feel more optimistic.

30 DAYS OF MORNING REFLECTION PRACTICE

Day 1
Day 2
Day 3

30 DAYS OF MORNING REFLECTION PRACTICE

Day 4
Day 5
Day 6

30 DAYS OF MORNING REFLECTION PRACTICE

Day 7

Day 8

Day 9

30 DAYS OF MORNING REFLECTION PRACTICE

Day 10
Day 11
Day 12

30 DAYS OF MORNING REFLECTION PRACTICE

Day 13
Day 14
Day 15

30 DAYS OF MORNING REFLECTION PRACTICE

Day 16
Day 17
Day 18

30 DAYS OF MORNING REFLECTION PRACTICE

Day 19
Day 20
Day 21

30 DAYS OF MORNING REFLECTION PRACTICE

Day 22
Day 23
Day 24

30 DAYS OF MORNING REFLECTION PRACTICE

Day 25
Day 26
Day 27

30 DAYS OF MORNING REFLECTION PRACTICE

Day 28
Day 29
Day 30

6. Mindful Awareness Planning (MAP)

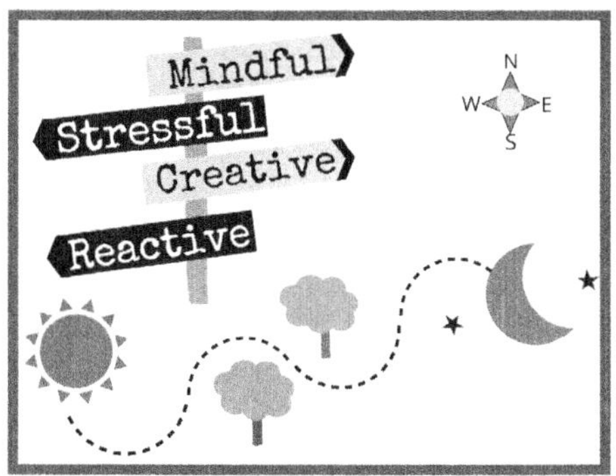

If you think of each day as a car journey, Mindful Awareness Planning (MAP) is simply a way to plan your route at the start of each day. It allows you to choose your destination and give yourself the guidance you need to get there. Don't leave your life to chance, create a MAP so you can live more intentionally and take back creative control over the direction each day takes.

TIP: Once you start living more intentionally you may find you don't need to write down your MAP as it becomes an automatic habit. Though you may decide to revisit it if your routine is disrupted so you can get back on track.

Why this works

Creating a Mindfulness Awareness Plan each day will encourage you to live intentionally and in alignment with what you want. It will help you avoid stress and reactivity by encouraging you to bring conscious intention to your day. You may not be able to control what happens to you every day, but using a MAP will help you take back some control over how you respond to it, which means you're less likely to get thrown off track.

Create a Mindful Awareness Plan for your day

Use the templates on pages 90–103 to create your MAP. There are two weeks' worth though if your weekdays are similar, you can use the same MAP for each weekday and only change it at the weekend.

- You can either complete your MAP in the morning (if you have time) or in the evening (in preparation for the next day).
- Spend a few minutes reflecting on your daily MAP before you start your day and keep referring to it so you stay on track.

How to create and use your MAP

Use the templates included on pages 90-103 to write out a plan for your ideal day.

- Divide your time into sections and think about what you want to bring to each period of your day. You can complete the MAP the night before if that's easier for you.
- Refer to your MAP for guidance throughout the day.
- You can reuse the same MAP or create a different one each day depending on what works for you.

EXAMPLE OF A MINDFUL AWARENESS PLAN (MAP)

TIME	ACTIVITY	INTENTION
7.00	Wake up	Come into the present and break my thoughts around the past or future.
7.30	Breakfast	Eat mindfully, stopping when I'm full and staying focused on the present
8.15	Leave for work	Arrive on time and safely at work and have a happy and calm journey.
9.00	Start work	Look for positives and things to be grateful for in my work environment.
11.00	At work	Bring awareness to mindful communication.
12.30	Lunch break	Do a mindful reset by going for a walk and getting back into the present moment.
3 pm	Afternoon slump	Do some yawning and stretching to reset and get back on track.
5.30	Leave work	Safe and calm journey home, finding compassion for other commuters.
6.30pm	Dinner	Find some joy in preparing food and express gratitude for having it.
8pm	Me time	Deliberately take some time to do something just for me - without any guilt.
9pm	Journalling	Getting stuff out of my head before bed to let it go and release the day.
10.30pm	Bedtime	Progressive muscle relaxation to prepare for a great night's sleep.

MINDFUL AWARENESS PLAN

TIME	ACTIVITY	INTENTION

MINDFUL AWARENESS PLAN

TIME	ACTIVITY	INTENTION

MINDFUL AWARENESS PLAN

TIME	ACTIVITY	INTENTION

MINDFUL AWARENESS PLAN

TIME	ACTIVITY	INTENTION

MINDFUL AWARENESS PLAN

TIME	ACTIVITY	INTENTION

MINDFUL AWARENESS PLAN

TIME	ACTIVITY	INTENTION

MINDFUL AWARENESS PLAN

TIME	ACTIVITY	INTENTION

MINDFUL AWARENESS PLAN

TIME	ACTIVITY	INTENTION

MINDFUL AWARENESS PLAN

TIME	ACTIVITY	INTENTION

MINDFUL AWARENESS PLAN

TIME	ACTIVITY	INTENTION

MINDFUL AWARENESS PLAN

TIME	ACTIVITY	INTENTION

MINDFUL AWARENESS PLAN

TIME	ACTIVITY	INTENTION

MINDFUL AWARENESS PLAN

TIME	ACTIVITY	INTENTION

MINDFUL AWARENESS PLAN

TIME	ACTIVITY	INTENTION

7. Positive Focus Tracker

A positive focus tracker is a great tool for helping you stay motivated. Using the templates on pages 107–120 you can bring mindful awareness to the activities that bring you joy and keep you motivated to reach your goals. You can either do this every day for a week or two, or whenever you want to shift your focus in a more positive direction. Here are some examples of activities that can help with positive focus:

- Music – Music can have an instant impact on our mood. It can energise us and bring back happy memories. It can also make us sad, so make sure you choose well! This is why having playlists on hand that suit different moods can be helpful.
- People – Spending time with or talking to people who inspire you is another way to keep your momentum going through the day. Even if you can't connect with others personally, try listening to podcasts to get ideas from others and stay motivated.
- Nature – Exercise and connecting with nature can boost your mind as well as your body.
- Nutrition – Good nutrition can also contribute to your health and well-being as it helps you maintain your energy levels and mental clarity. Also consider how you are nourishing your mind. It's beneficial to be a conscious consumer of information as well as food.
- Creativity – Any creative pursuits such as painting, writing, drawing, cooking, gardening, playing instruments, reading, even practising sports can help you feel inspired and motivated. Not only can you enjoy the activity, but you'll be motivated as you see your skills improve.
- Mindfulness – Any mindful practice will bring you back to the present moment, helping you stay focused and aware. Meditation is especially effective so it's worth making time for it.

Why this works

By bringing awareness to positive things happening around us we start to notice more of them which helps lift our mood. Having a list of 'go-to' activities that motivate and inspire us helps maintain our motivation to reach our goals. By writing these down on the tracker, we start to understand to which ones work the best for us.

EXAMPLE OF A COMPLETED POSITIVE FOCUS TRACKER

DATE: 12/4

TIME	MOOD BEFORE SCALE: 0-10	WHAT WAS THE POSITIVE EVENT/ ACTIVITY?	MOOD AFTER SCALE: 0-10
7.30 am	4	Noticed sunrise.	6 - lifted my spirits.
8.30 am	6	Good journey, other cars let me go, I did the same.	8 - felt good to help others.
10.15 am	7	Helped a work colleague with a difficult task.	8 - felt positive about work.
5.30 pm	5	Decided to enjoy the journey home, sang along in the car.	8 - music always uplifts me.
7.15 pm	5	Got a hug from my kids and petted my dog.	8 - grateful for the love I have in my life.

How to use the Positive Focus Tracker

Fill out the trackers on the following pages to help you notice what objects, events and activities bring you joy. The mood scale is optional, so if you don't want to spend too much time on this simply write down the positive event.

Mood before positive event

Noticing the mood you were in before the positive event helps you recognise how both your emotional state and the event itself affect your wellbeing.

- 0 = low mood, e.g. tired/depressed.
- 10 = high mood, e.g. excited/optimistic.

Mood after positive event

- 0 = no difference
- 10 = very positive

POSITIVE FOCUS TRACKER

DATE:

TIME	MOOD BEFORE SCALE: 0-10	WHAT WAS THE POSITIVE EVENT/ ACTIVITY?	MOOD AFTER SCALE: 0-10

POSITIVE FOCUS TRACKER

DATE:

TIME	MOOD BEFORE SCALE: 0-10	WHAT WAS THE POSITIVE EVENT/ ACTIVITY?	MOOD AFTER SCALE: 0-10

POSITIVE FOCUS TRACKER

DATE:

TIME	MOOD BEFORE SCALE: 0-10	WHAT WAS THE POSITIVE EVENT/ ACTIVITY?	MOOD AFTER SCALE: 0-10

POSITIVE FOCUS TRACKER

DATE:

TIME	MOOD BEFORE SCALE: 0-10	WHAT WAS THE POSITIVE EVENT/ ACTIVITY?	MOOD AFTER SCALE: 0-10

POSITIVE FOCUS TRACKER

DATE:

TIME	MOOD BEFORE SCALE: 0-10	WHAT WAS THE POSITIVE EVENT/ ACTIVITY?	MOOD AFTER SCALE: 0-10

POSITIVE FOCUS TRACKER

DATE:

TIME	MOOD BEFORE SCALE: 0-10	WHAT WAS THE POSITIVE EVENT/ ACTIVITY?	MOOD AFTER SCALE: 0-10

POSITIVE FOCUS TRACKER

DATE:

TIME	MOOD BEFORE SCALE: 0-10	WHAT WAS THE POSITIVE EVENT/ ACTIVITY?	MOOD AFTER SCALE: 0-10

POSITIVE FOCUS TRACKER

DATE:

TIME	MOOD BEFORE SCALE: 0-10	WHAT WAS THE POSITIVE EVENT/ ACTIVITY?	MOOD AFTER SCALE: 0-10

POSITIVE FOCUS TRACKER

DATE:

TIME	MOOD BEFORE SCALE: 0-10	WHAT WAS THE POSITIVE EVENT/ ACTIVITY?	MOOD AFTER SCALE: 0-10

POSITIVE FOCUS TRACKER

DATE:

TIME	MOOD BEFORE SCALE: 0-10	WHAT WAS THE POSITIVE EVENT/ ACTIVITY?	MOOD AFTER SCALE: 0-10

POSITIVE FOCUS TRACKER

DATE:

TIME	MOOD BEFORE SCALE: 0-10	WHAT WAS THE POSITIVE EVENT/ ACTIVITY?	MOOD AFTER SCALE: 0-10

POSITIVE FOCUS TRACKER

DATE:

TIME	MOOD BEFORE SCALE: 0-10	WHAT WAS THE POSITIVE EVENT/ ACTIVITY?	MOOD AFTER SCALE: 0-10

POSITIVE FOCUS TRACKER

DATE:

TIME	MOOD BEFORE SCALE: 0-10	WHAT WAS THE POSITIVE EVENT/ ACTIVITY?	MOOD AFTER SCALE: 0-10

POSITIVE FOCUS TRACKER

DATE:

TIME	MOOD BEFORE SCALE: 0-10	WHAT WAS THE POSITIVE EVENT/ ACTIVITY?	MOOD AFTER SCALE: 0-10

ONGOING PRACTICE

One way to make sustainable changes is to adopt long-term practices that can support you in building new habits. Journalling is a great way to do this. Although you can journal at any time of the day, most people tend to choose either the morning or the evening. In this workbook, there are two different types of journalling: Intention Setting Journalling for the morning and Reflective journalling for the evening.

8. Intention Setting Journalling

The morning journalling practice is for intention setting. Look through the example on the next page to see how to do it then use the fourteen days of blank templates for practice. There are more blank journal templates at the end of the workbook. They're divided into morning and evening pages so you can combine the two journalling practices.

If you want to continue your journalling practice, use the *Micro Mindfulness: Intention Setting Journal*, which accompanies this workbook.

EXAMPLE OF A COMPLETED INTENTION SETTING JOURNAL PAGE

Date: 01/05/20

Current emotion: Anxiety

Desired emotion: Empowerment

Today's Values List	
1. Family	4. Creativity
2. Freedom	5. Joy
3. Love	6. Peace

Today's Affirmation
"I let go of the past with love and embrace the future with excitement."

Today's Positive Focus Activity
Listen to music/podcasts that inspire me. Journal for 20 minutes. Go for a mindful walk in nature.

Today's Goals/Intentions
Commute mindfully and stay calm. Make an effort to get on with work colleagues. Eat a healthy lunch.

MORNING MOTIVATION

Date: ______________________________

Current emotion: ______________________________

Desired emotion: ______________________________

Today's Values List

1.
2.
3.
4.
5.
6.

Today's Affirmation

Today's Positive Focus Activity

Today's Goals / Intentions

MORNING MOTIVATION

Date: ______________________________

Current emotion: ______________________________

Desired emotion: ______________________________

Today's Values List	
1.	4.
2.	5.
3.	6.

Today's Affirmation

Today's Positive Focus Activity

Today's Goals / Intentions

MORNING MOTIVATION

Date: ____________________

Current emotion: ____________________

Desired emotion: ____________________

Today's Values List	
1.	4.
2.	5.
3.	6.

Today's Affirmation

Today's Positive Focus Activity

Today's Goals / Intentions

MORNING MOTIVATION

Date: ______________________________

Current emotion: ______________________________

Desired emotion: ______________________________

Today's Values List	
1.	4.
2.	5.
3.	6.

Today's Affirmation

Today's Positive Focus Activity

Today's Goals / Intentions

MORNING MOTIVATION

Date: ______________________________

Current emotion: ______________________________

Desired emotion: ______________________________

Today's Values List	
1.	4.
2.	5.
3.	6.

Today's Affirmation

Today's Positive Focus Activity

Today's Goals / Intentions

MORNING MOTIVATION

Date: ______________________________

Current emotion: ______________________________

Desired emotion: ______________________________

Today's Values List	
1.	4.
2.	5.
3.	6.

Today's Affirmation

Today's Positive Focus Activity

Today's Goals / Intentions

MORNING MOTIVATION

Date: ______________________________

Current emotion: ______________________________

Desired emotion: ______________________________

Today's Values List	
1.	4.
2.	5.
3.	6.

Today's Affirmation

Today's Positive Focus Activity

Today's Goals / Intentions

MORNING MOTIVATION

Date: ______________________________

Current emotion: ______________________________

Desired emotion: ______________________________

Today's Values List	
1.	4.
2.	5.
3.	6.

Today's Affirmation

Today's Positive Focus Activity

Today's Goals / Intentions

MORNING MOTIVATION

Date: ____________________

Current emotion: ____________________

Desired emotion: ____________________

Today's Values List	
1.	4.
2.	5.
3.	6.

Today's Affirmation

Today's Positive Focus Activity

Today's Goals / Intentions

MORNING MOTIVATION

Date: ______________________________

Current emotion: ______________________________

Desired emotion: ______________________________

Today's Values List	
1.	4.
2.	5.
3.	6.

Today's Affirmation

Today's Positive Focus Activity

Today's Goals / Intentions

MORNING MOTIVATION

Date: ____________________________

Current emotion: ____________________________

Desired emotion: ____________________________

Today's Values List	
1.	4.
2.	5.
3.	6.

Today's Affirmation

Today's Positive Focus Activity

Today's Goals / Intentions

MORNING MOTIVATION

Date: ______________________________

Current emotion: ______________________________

Desired emotion: ______________________________

Today's Values List	
1.	4.
2.	5.
3.	6.

Today's Affirmation

Today's Positive Focus Activity

Today's Goals / Intentions

MORNING MOTIVATION

Date: ________________________________

Current emotion: ________________________________

Desired emotion: ________________________________

Today's Values List	
1.	4.
2.	5.
3.	6.

Today's Affirmation

Today's Positive Focus Activity

Today's Goals / Intentions

MORNING MOTIVATION

Date: ______________________________

Current emotion: ______________________________

Desired emotion: ______________________________

Today's Values List	
1.	4.
2.	5.
3.	6.

Today's Affirmation

Today's Positive Focus Activity

Today's Goals / Intentions

PART TWO

REFLECTIVE EVENINGS

GET READY FOR A GOOD NIGHT'S SLEEP

These exercises have been designed to help you unwind, reflect and process the day, so you get a great night's sleep!

If you do this therapeutic practice long-term it'll help you stay on track with your mindfulness habits. You can use your own journal, or the templates on pages 158–171 or in the *Micro Mindfulness: Intention Setting Journal*, which has been designed to accompany this workbook.

EXERCISE CHECKLIST

Habit-forming exercise

9. 21 Days of Gratitude

Ongoing practice

10. Reflective Journalling

HABIT-FORMING EXERCISE

Any exercise that helps you form a habit is useful because habits are automatic behaviours. That means you'll do certain things without having to remember them or plan to do them. One of the most valuable habits you can develop is gratitude. It's especially valuable to do gratitude practice in the evening as you look back and reflect on your day. It's all too easy to focus on the negative aspects of your day, but practising gratitude means you automatically focus on the positive.

9. 21 Days of Gratitude

Gratitude has such a positive impact on our emotions that it's well worth starting a regular gratitude practice. Commit to doing it for a period of time so you integrate it into your daily routine. Bear in mind that it might sometimes feel hard to find things to be grateful for, so go easy on yourself when you first start.

Aim to make this practice fun and interesting but most of all, make it work for you. If you're feeling down or demotivated you might not be in the right frame of mind to do this. In that case, you can either wait until you feel more like doing it or simply repeat the words 'thank you' as a mantra. You might find it jogs you into noticing things to be thankful for.

Why this works

What we focus on dominates our lives, but unfortunately, we tend to spend more time focusing on what we don't want, what has gone wrong or what might go wrong in the future than on what we want. Gratitude encourages us to focus on what is positive and what went right in the past. It helps us to appreciate what we have and look forward to the future with more optimism. Developing the habit of gratitude helps us notice more of what is going well for us rather than what hasn't worked.

EXAMPLE OF COMPLETED GRATITUDE PRACTICE DIARY

Day 1

I'm so grateful for the experiences I've had in my life because they've brought me to this point. Although it didn't seem like it at the time, I needed to face those challenges. If I hadn't, I wouldn't be the person I am today.

I'm grateful for the supportive people I have in my life.

I'm grateful for my health and that I am able to walk outside and enjoy nature.

Day 2

I feel blessed that I'm able to share my knowledge with others, especially those who are suffering.

I'm grateful for the teachers who've helped me see where I'm not loving myself enough.

I'm grateful for my love of reading and cooking, both bring me such joy.

I'm grateful for all the wonderful music I have access to as it can lift my mood in an instant.

How to practise 21 Days of Gratitude

Refer to the sample gratitude practice on page 141. Next, follow the guide below and use the blank templates on pages 143–153 to start your own gratitude practice.

- Every day, write down at least one thing – and ideally six or more things – you're grateful for. If you struggle, build up gradually over time.
- Use the gratitude prompts below to get started or think up your own questions to encourage feelings of gratitude.

Gratitude Prompts

- Name someone or something you're grateful for and say why.
- Recall a happy memory of a person, item or event you're grateful for.
- Write about an accomplishment you're proud of achieving.
- Think about something you are looking forward to?
- What aspect of your health are you grateful for?
- What have you been given that you're grateful for?
- Which artist, musician or author's work are you grateful for?
- Think of a time when you helped someone. How did that make you feel?
- List your strengths and say why you're grateful for them.
- What do you own that makes your life easier?
- Write about the life experiences (good or bad) that you are grateful for and why?

21 DAYS OF GRATITUDE

Day 1

Day 2

21 DAYS OF GRATITUDE

Day 3

Day 4

21 DAYS OF GRATITUDE

Day 5

Day 6

21 DAYS OF GRATITUDE

Day 7

Day 8

21 DAYS OF GRATITUDE

Day 9

Day 10

21 DAYS OF GRATITUDE

Day 11

Day 12

21 DAYS OF GRATITUDE

Day 13

Day 14

21 DAYS OF GRATITUDE

Day 15

Day 16

21 DAYS OF GRATITUDE

Day 17

Day 18

21 DAYS OF GRATITUDE

Day 19

Day 20

21 DAYS OF GRATITUDE

Day 21

ONGOING PRACTICE

10. Reflective Journalling

Reflective journalling is a therapeutic tool that helps you reflect back on your day (or a recent life event) allowing you to get more clarity on how you managed it. It encourages a shift in perspective, helping you become an objective observer of past events rather than getting bogged down in the emotions associated with them. Reflecting on past experiences will help you work out what triggers you, as well as giving you the chance to consider how you could better manage similar situations in the future. The Rewrite Your Day exercise can be combined with daily journalling to help you get more out of the practice.

How to practise reflective journalling

If you wish, you can adapt this practice to give you time to reflect on a specific life event rather than your usual daily events. Don't beat yourself up about what you might have got wrong, acknowledge that you did the best you could given the information you had at the time then forgive yourself and move on.

- Write about what happened during the day from the perspective of a dispassionate observer.
- Put the events into chronological order and do your best to stick to the facts so you can remain objective.
- Consider what went right or wrong and think about what you might do differently next time.

Why this works

Journalling is a great tool for getting things out of our heads and onto paper. When we write out our thoughts, it's much easier to be objective and helps us get a better perspective on situations. We can also be more honest when we write as we don't have to worry about the emotional response of others.

EXAMPLE OF A COMPLETED EVENING REFLECTION JOURNAL PAGE

Listening to music and podcasts while I walked really helped lift my mood today. I am going to try to do this every day.

Looking back, I realise that I spent too much time on social media today and that made me feel negative. So, I'm going to incorporate a digital detox into my routine to see if that helps me stay more positive.

I had a positive day at work giving advice to customers. I made an effort to be as helpful as possible. People were grateful for my expertise and efforts. It feels good to be needed. I also had a good journey home listening to upbeat music.

I'm grateful for my job, my relationships, my home and my health.

I'm grateful that I've lived to see another day on this amazing planet when not everyone is so fortunate. It reminds me that life is a gift.

I'm looking forward to seeing what tomorrow brings.

How to rewrite your day

This is a good exercise to do when you want to switch from a negative to a positive mindset so you feel better emotionally. As humans, our memories are flawed and we often remember what has happened incorrectly. We also have a tendency to place greater emphasis on what went wrong rather than what went right. This practice is a great way to change that. It's worth remembering that the more reflective journalling you do, the more you'll focus on the positive aspects of your day rather than the negative.

- If you've had a bad day, try rewriting it as if it was either a good day or the day you wish you'd had. How does focusing on this new version of your day change how you feel?
- Use this rewritten version to develop strategies for creating better days in the future.
- You can also incorporate some gratitude journalling into your practice developed in the 21 Days of Gratitude exercise.

Why this works

Rewriting your day helps to shift your focus away from what you think went wrong to a more objective view. This enables you to move on faster and can give you ideas about what changes you want to make to create better days in the future.

Please remember…

While journalling is a useful therapeutic tool, it is just a tool and isn't a replacement for proper therapy. If you are suffering from any kind of trauma, you should seek professional advice and help.

EXAMPLE OF HOW TO REWRITE YOUR DAY

Reflection on a stressful day

Customers were rude all day and I was bombarded with email complaints. My colleagues were all stressed too, so the atmosphere was really unpleasant. Everyone was snapping at each other. My commute home was awful, which made me feel even more stressed. I took it out on my partner when I got home and we ended up arguing. I'm now feeling really tired, stressed and fed up.

Rewritten with a positive mindset

Got the opportunity to help out lots of customers and help resolve their problems. I am so grateful that I have the chance to help people as part of my job.

I saw that some of my colleagues were feeling stressed, so made time to talk to them and find out what was wrong. I think that made a big difference to their day.

It was a busy commute home and I'm glad I had some great music to listen to. Making the most of this time to myself helped me chill out, so by the time I got home I was feeling calm. I had a relaxed evening with my partner.

I'm now feeling reenergised and ready for tomorrow.

EVENING REFLECTION

- What worked and will I change?
- Rewrite my day
- Gratitude journalling

EVENING REFLECTION

- What worked and will I change?
- Rewrite my day
- Gratitude journalling

EVENING REFLECTION

- What worked and will I change?
- Rewrite my day
- Gratitude journalling

EVENING REFLECTION

- What worked and will I change?
- Rewrite my day
- Gratitude journalling

EVENING REFLECTION

- What worked and will I change?
- Rewrite my day
- Gratitude journalling

EVENING REFLECTION

- What worked and will I change?
- Rewrite my day
- Gratitude journalling

EVENING REFLECTION

- What worked and will I change?
- Rewrite my day
- Gratitude journalling

EVENING REFLECTION

- What worked and will I change?
- Rewrite my day
- Gratitude journalling

EVENING REFLECTION

- What worked and will I change?
- Rewrite my day
- Gratitude journalling

EVENING REFLECTION

- What worked and will I change?
- Rewrite my day
- Gratitude journalling

EVENING REFLECTION

- What worked and will I change?
- Rewrite my day
- Gratitude journalling

EVENING REFLECTION

- What worked and will I change?
- Rewrite my day
- Gratitude journalling

EVENING REFLECTION

- What worked and will I change?
- Rewrite my day
- Gratitude journalling

EVENING REFLECTION

- What worked and will I change?
- Rewrite my day
- Gratitude journalling

PART 3

BRINGING IT ALL TOGETHER

JOURNALLING PRACTICE

Journalling and reflective practice are great mindful habits that help you focus on what you want more of in your life while releasing what you don't. You get the best results when you practise both morning and evening journalling because together they combine all the wellbeing habits laid out in this workbook to create a manageable daily practice.

> **Why this works**
>
> *While keeping an intention setting journal helps you start your day the right way, the evening reflective practice allows you to release emotions and prepare for a better day tomorrow. By reflecting on what has and hasn't worked today, you can prepare to do, be and have more of what you want. As you gradually become more focused on what works, it becomes easier to develop the habits that support this new way of living.*

14 DAYS OF JOURNALLING

On the following pages, there are 14 days' worth of morning and evening journalling pages for you to practise with. If you want to continue with this practice beyond 14 days, you can either use your own journal or the *Micro Mindfulness: Intention Setting Journal*, which has been designed to accompany this workbook. As you continue to practise what you've learned in this workbook, remember that when you create better moments, you create better days, which creates a better life. That's what micro mindfulness is all about.

DAY 1: MORNING MOTIVATION

Date: ______________________________

Current emotion: ______________________________

Desired emotion: ______________________________

Today's Values List	
1.	4.
2.	5.
3.	6.

Today's Affirmation

Today's Positive Focus Activity

Today's Goals / Intentions

EVENING REFLECTION

- What worked and will I change?
- Rewrite my day
- Gratitude journalling

DAY 2: MORNING MOTIVATION

Date: ______________________________

Current emotion: ______________________________

Desired emotion: ______________________________

Today's Values List	
1.	4.
2.	5.
3.	6.

Today's Affirmation

Today's Positive Focus Activity

Today's Goals / Intentions

EVENING REFLECTION

- What worked and will I change?
- Rewrite my day
- Gratitude journalling

DAY 3: MORNING MOTIVATION

Date: ______________________________

Current emotion: ______________________________

Desired emotion: ______________________________

Today's Values List	
1.	4.
2.	5.
3.	6.

Today's Affirmation

Today's Positive Focus Activity

Today's Goals / Intentions

EVENING REFLECTION

- What worked and will I change?
- Rewrite my day
- Gratitude journalling

DAY 4: MORNING MOTIVATION

Date: ______________________________

Current emotion: ______________________________

Desired emotion: ______________________________

Today's Values List	
1.	4.
2.	5.
3.	6.

Today's Affirmation

Today's Positive Focus Activity

Today's Goals / Intentions

EVENING REFLECTION

- What worked and will I change?
- Rewrite my day
- Gratitude journalling

DAY 5: MORNING MOTIVATION

Date: ______________________________

Current emotion: ______________________________

Desired emotion: ______________________________

Today's Values List	
1.	4.
2.	5.
3.	6.

Today's Affirmation

Today's Positive Focus Activity

Today's Goals / Intentions

EVENING REFLECTION

- What worked and will I change?
- Rewrite my day
- Gratitude journalling

DAY 6: MORNING MOTIVATION

Date: ____________________

Current emotion: ____________________

Desired emotion: ____________________

Today's Values List	
1.	4.
2.	5.
3.	6.

Today's Affirmation

Today's Positive Focus Activity

Today's Goals / Intentions

EVENING REFLECTION

- What worked and will I change?
- Rewrite my day
- Gratitude journalling

DAY 7: MORNING MOTIVATION

Date: ______________________________

Current emotion: ______________________________

Desired emotion: ______________________________

Today's Values List	
1.	4.
2.	5.
3.	6.

Today's Affirmation

Today's Positive Focus Activity

Today's Goals / Intentions

EVENING REFLECTION

- What worked and will I change?
- Rewrite my day
- Gratitude journalling

DAY 8: MORNING MOTIVATION

Date: ______________________________

Current emotion: ______________________________

Desired emotion: ______________________________

Today's Values List	
1.	4.
2.	5.
3.	6.

Today's Affirmation

Today's Positive Focus Activity

Today's Goals / Intentions

EVENING REFLECTION

- What worked and will I change?
- Rewrite my day
- Gratitude journalling

DAY 9: MORNING MOTIVATION

Date: ______________________________

Current emotion: ______________________________

Desired emotion: ______________________________

Today's Values List	
1.	4.
2.	5.
3.	6.

Today's Affirmation

Today's Positive Focus Activity

Today's Goals / Intentions

EVENING REFLECTION

- What worked and will I change?
- Rewrite my day
- Gratitude journalling

DAY 10: MORNING MOTIVATION

Date: ______________________________

Current emotion: ______________________________

Desired emotion: ______________________________

Today's Values List	
1.	4.
2.	5.
3.	6.

Today's Affirmation

Today's Positive Focus Activity

Today's Goals / Intentions

EVENING REFLECTION

- What worked and will I change?
- Rewrite my day
- Gratitude journalling

DAY 11: MORNING MOTIVATION

Date: ______________________________

Current emotion: ______________________________

Desired emotion: ______________________________

Today's Values List	
1.	4.
2.	5.
3.	6.

Today's Affirmation

Today's Positive Focus Activity

Today's Goals / Intentions

EVENING REFLECTION

- What worked and will I change?
- Rewrite my day
- Gratitude journalling

DAY 12: MORNING MOTIVATION

Date: ______________________________

Current emotion: ______________________________

Desired emotion: ______________________________

Today's Values List	
1.	4.
2.	5.
3.	6.

Today's Affirmation

Today's Positive Focus Activity

Today's Goals / Intentions

EVENING REFLECTION

- What worked and will I change?
- Rewrite my day
- Gratitude journalling

DAY 13: MORNING MOTIVATION

Date: ______________________________

Current emotion: ______________________________

Desired emotion: ______________________________

Today's Values List	
1.	4.
2.	5.
3.	6.

Today's Affirmation

Today's Positive Focus Activity

Today's Goals / Intentions

EVENING REFLECTION

- What worked and will I change?
- Rewrite my day
- Gratitude journalling

DAY 14: MORNING MOTIVATION

Date: ______________________________

Current emotion: ______________________________

Desired emotion: ______________________________

Today's Values List	
1.	4.
2.	5.
3.	6.

Today's Affirmation

Today's Positive Focus Activity

Today's Goals / Intentions

EVENING REFLECTION

- What worked and will I change?
- Rewrite my day
- Gratitude journalling

NEXT STEPS

The mindful practices in this workbook provide some great tools to help you live more intentionally and reflectively, but did you know there are many ways of incorporating some mini mindful moments into your daily routine?

If you've enjoyed using this workbook and would like to know more about mindfulness and the micro mindful hacks you can incorporate into your daily life, please feel free to check out the book, *Micro Mindfulness: Mini Mindful Hacks* or the *Micro Mindfulness: Intention Setting Journal* designed to accompany this workbook so you can start creating the life you want one micro-mindful moment at a time.

Good luck on your journey and wherever it takes you. I hope this workbook helps you to get there more mindfully!

Printed in Great Britain
by Amazon

85408681R00122